# THE ASIAN RENAISSANCE

Project Editor: Christine Chua
Art Director: Tuck Loong
Production Manager: Anthoney Chua
Cover Photography: Mark Law


© 1996 Anwar Ibrahim

Published by Times Books International
An imprint of Times Editions Pte Ltd
Times Centre
1 New Industrial Road
Singapore 536196
Fax: (65) 285 4871
Tel: (65) 284 8844
e-mail: te@corp.tpl.com.sg

Times Subang
Lot 46, Subang Hi-Tech Industrial Park
Batu Tiga
40000 Shah Alam
Selangor Darul Ehsan
Malaysia
Fax and Tel: (603) 736 3517

Reprinted 1997 (twice)

Printed by Times Offset (M) Sdn. Bhd.

ISBN 981 204 783 2 (standard edition)
ISBN 981 204 784 0 (deluxe edition)
ISBN 981 204 785 9 (limited edition)

# THE ASIAN
# RENAISSANCE

TIMES BOOKS INTERNATIONAL
*Singapore • Kuala Lumpur*

*To my father and mother*

# Contents

# Preface

The central theme of this book represents an idea that has been germinating in my mind for some time. Over the past decade, scores of books have been written on the rise of East Asia. Most of them, however, focused almost exclusively on the economic revolution that has freed millions from abject poverty and transformed East Asia into a dynamo powering the global economy. A new phrase was even coined to encapsulate this revolution: The East Asian Economic Miracle.

This phenomenon has given rise to the self-induced fear on the part of the West that its civilization is on the verge of being overwhelmed by a horde of marauding Asians. This portrayal of Asia demonstrates that little has changed over centuries in the way the West perceives Asia. The fact remains that the West still continues to dominate the world economically, culturally and politically.

Asia's economic progress is, in fact, a boon because it has enabled Asia to rediscover its soul and to reconstruct its civilizations. Inevitably this process will necessitate civilizational dialogue between the East and the West.

The main ideas in this book have been expounded in speeches made over the last several years in the course of my various engagements in the region and in the West.

Many of the thoughts expressed in *Symbiosis Between East and West* were articulated for the first time at Georgetown University, Washington D.C., in October 1994. The presence of Muslim and Christian scholars gave me the opportunity to make a call for civilizational dialogue between East and West. These ideas have been reiterated in subsequent forums such as the Islam-Confucianism Dialogue in Kuala Lumpur in 1995 and a speech at the Ateneo de Manila University in the Philippines in May 1996.

The concept of civil society and democracy, the theme of my speech in Bangkok in September 1994 and of a lecture at the Johns Hopkins University, Washington D.C., in October 1995, has now found its way into the essay *Democracy and Civil Society*, along with other issues of the day.

The essays, *Ethics and Economics* and *The Humane Economy*, are largely based on a speech delivered at the Royal Institute of International Affairs, Chatham House, London, in July 1996 and Budget speeches in the Malaysian parliament.

*Islam in Southeast Asia* has its genesis in an essay published in the 23 September 1996 issue of *Time* magazine. Likewise, the concluding chapter, *The Asia of the Future*, is an expanded version of my essay in the 50th Anniversary Commemorative issue of the *Far Eastern Economic Review*. Edited versions of several speeches have appeared in the *International Herald Tribune* and various editions of the *Wall Street Journal*.

The opening essay, *An Asian Renaissance*, cannot be pigeon-holed into any particular speech or previously published essay because it forms the central thesis of my vision for Asia. This theme has been repeated in the various speeches and articles as well as throughout the book.

The ideas in this book are the product of personal reflections on events, writings and encounters with personalities. Religious upbringing, customs and traditional practices in the kampung have nurtured in me a profound sense of cultural rootedness. But that has not prevented me from forging lasting friendships with people of other backgrounds, races, cultures and faiths. I still remember how, as a child, I used to read with enthusiasm Asian history and literature, autobiographies and the Books of Mencius, from a small collection of my father's, and taking copious notes in the process. Exposure to the English public school tradition at the Malay College Kuala Kangsar in the 1960s enabled me to gain familiarity with the English language, its literature and the thoughts of its great writers. My past involvement in youth movements has enabled me to meet and fraternize with people of diverse backgrounds, races and beliefs. This has imbued in me not merely a strong sense of tolerance for others but a sincere and fervent belief that all of us belong to only one community and that is the universal community of mankind.

I grew up in a time of great social transformation wherein the interplay of ideas and events coincided with the rise of student activism, religious revivalism and political turmoil. Not content to be a mere bystander, I chose to be an active participant instead. I emerged from all this convinced that, while a life of contemplation and solitude can indeed be invigorating to the mind and the soul, a life of contemplation coupled with action and fraternity can be even more so. I have no regrets for the road not taken because the one that I took has led me to a challenging and fulfilling public life. And it is in this domain that I will continue to actively and fully participate in the realization of the higher ideals of life. What these ideals are, this book will attempt to elucidate.

I am indebted in a very special way to Dr Mahathir Mohamad for the writing of this book. For his tolerance and for his giving me the latitude to articulate my thoughts, I am indeed grateful. I thank my friends who have assisted me in completing this book, and the publishers for their indulgence.

Finally, my heartfelt appreciation to my wife, Wan Azizah, and our children, for their love, patience and understanding. Without them life itself would be bereft of joy and happiness.

Kuala Lumpur
December 1996

# An Asian Renaissance

The rise of Asia as the centre of global economic activity has been sudden and profound. Twenty-five years ago, Asian countries were still struggling to attain political stability, having been an arena for superpower rivalry since the end of the Second World War. Today, when much of the rest of the world is labouring under a cloud of pessimism, Asia is fired by a new sense of confidence. Japan has tilted the balance of economic might; Asean and the Newly Industrializing Countries (NICs) continue to surge ahead in prosperity; China, once dubbed by Napoleon as the sleeping giant, has finally awakened; South Asia is already on the growth bandwagon and the countries of Indochina are rebuilding their economies.

The economic rise of Asia, though critical and fundamental, is only a dimension of a much deeper, more profound and far-reaching reawakening of the continent which may be called the Asian Renaissance. By Asian Renaissance we mean the revival of the arts and sciences under the influence of classical models based on strong moral and religious foundations; a cultural resurgence dominated by a reflowering of art and literature, architecture and music and advancements in science and technology.

In the case of the European (Florentine) Renaissance between the fourteenth and sixteenth centuries, where "intellectual enfranchisement and moral release" was the cornerstone, the intense assertion of the power of the individual to determine his own destiny led to the flourishing of secular humanism at the expense of Judeo-Christian religiosity. As Will Durant wrote: "The brilliant enfranchisement of the mind sapped the supernatural sanctions of morality, and no others were found to effectually replace them. The result was such a repudiation of inhibitions, such a release of impulse and desire, so gay a luxuriance of immorality, as history had not known since the Sophists shattered the myths, freed the mind, and loosened the morals of ancient Greece."[1]

While sharing many similarities such as the recourse to the classical eras of the various Asian traditions, the Asian Renaissance, however, differs fundamentally from the European in that it has its foundations in religion and traditions – Islam, Confucianism, Buddhism, Hinduism and Christianity being the major ones.

European Renaissance thought resurrected the ancient myth of Prometheus in seeking an expression for its idea of Man. Prometheus, rather than being seen negatively as symbolizing Man's rebellion against Heaven, came to be cherished as an agent independent of the theological and natural order. This is diametrically opposed to, not only the Islamic concept of Man as God's vicegerent on Earth (*khalīfa Allāh fi'l-arḍ*) and the Confucian *jen*, but also the Christian concept of Man as *Imago Dei* or *Pontifex*, the bridge between Heaven and Earth.[2] Consequent upon this new vision of Man, the West began to sever itself from the dominant world view of the Age of Faith, a process which accelerated after the Enlightenment. On the other hand, Asia, despite centuries of change and transformation, retains its essential religious character. The Asian Man at heart is *persona religiosus*.

Spurred on by moral release, the European Renaissance became a movement to liberate the mind from the tyranny of organized control and became a pretext for anarchy and toleration of sensate culture. The renaissance of Asia, however, entails the growth, development and flowering of Asian societies based on a certain vision of perfection; societies imbued with truth and the love of learning, justice and compassion, mutual respect and forbearance, and freedom with responsibility. Faith and religious practice is not confined to the individual, it permeates the life of the community. It is religion rather than any other social force which makes Asia a continent of infinite diversity. Thus, the renewal of faith and the assertion of multiculturality is an integral component of the Asian Renaissance. Embodying this spirit of the Asian Renaissance, poet-philosopher Muhammad Iqbal (1873–1938) wrote:

> That I may lead home the wanderer
> And imbue the idle looker-on with restless impatience
> And advance hotly on a new quest,
> And become known as the champion of a new spirit.[3]

As the fresh blossoms of the Asian Renaissance are only beginning to appear, it is crucial that the nurturing process be sustained if it is to be brought to fruition. The task is rendered all the more challenging as we enter the twenty-first century, which certainly will be more complex and mystifying than the present one. It is only with a clear sense of direction and conviction that we may navigate the perils of the new millennium.

Undoubtedly, the issues are far from simple, but the current debate on the subject is mired in misunderstanding and prejudice, with one side fervently whitewashing Asia and the other constantly deprecating it. It is not simply a matter of pitting the virtues of Asia against the vices of the West.

## THE LURE OF JINGOISM

The multifaceted character of the European Renaissance, beyond the creation and enjoyment of the creative products of the mind, imagination and taste, has long been recognized. It was an entire society in transformation – its values, tastes, social etiquette, vision of the individual and collective destiny, attitude towards religion and morality. It was also the rise of "the state as a work of art"[4], the art of diplomacy, techniques of war, and the birth of patriotism. Likewise, the renaissance of Asia is the transformation of its cultures and societies from its capitulation to Atlantic powers to the position of self-confidence and its reflowering at the dawn of a new millennium. Bustling commerce and dynamic industries are the most visible aspects powering "the great ascent" and a revolution in the standard of living of its people. In an age where economic strength surpasses military might in the scale of importance, the voice of Asia can no longer be faint. A rediscovery of the idea of the dignity and sanctity of the human person, rooted in Asian traditions and in other traditions of mankind, will accelerate the growth of civil society and humane governance. In all these, Asia, perhaps humanity at large, will be enriched by the fruits of the life of the mind of its philosophers and the creative labour of its artists.

Being the cradle of several great civilizations, Asia is anything but monolithic. The Asian Renaissance must not be about cultural jingoism but rather about cultural rebirth and empowerment. Jingoism presupposes a sense of superiority of one's own culture over others, and with it, the connotation that others are less civilized, if at all. The offshoot is cultural imperialism. If allowed to spread, the flames of jingoism may eventually engulf Asians themselves. He who sows the wind, will reap the whirlwind. This is not a hypothetical issue but a stark reality. The fact is that there are Asian nations today still struggling to tame religious, ethnic and tribal hostilities within their boundaries.

In many developing societies, the pull of nativistic tendencies is ever present and often manifested with great beauty in works of art and literature. Faced with accelerated change, those unable to relate to new situations often withdraw into their ethnic cocoons. The spectre of these sentiments being mobilized into parochial and tribalistic political forces is indeed daunting. Not too long ago, the world bore witness to the destructive consequences of the revival of extreme ethnic and primitive passion in the Balkans, especially among the Serbs, and in Rwanda, between the Hutus and the Tutsis. Asians in the new century must avoid this danger at all cost. And this includes transcending their particularities to forge a new civilization upon what they already have in common and what they can make universal from their own specific experiences.

The progenitors and early protagonists of the Asian Renaissance such as José Rizal, Muhammad Iqbal and Rabindranath Tagore, were transmitters par excellence of the humanistic tradition. They not only fought for humanitarian ideals but also cultivated in their persons the life of the mind, the arts and imagination. They were able to transcend cultural specificity to inhabit the realm of universal ideas. They sought to reinvigorate the Asian self, fractured and deformed by colonialism. "Humanity will not be redeemed," Rizal wrote, "while reason is not free, while faith would want to impose itself against facts, while whims are laws and while there are nations that subjugate the others."[5]

To seek cultural empowerment is to bring ourselves up to a level of parity with other more self-confident cultures. It involves rediscovery of what has been forgotten through ages of weakness and decay; it involves renewal and reflowering. And it must inevitably involve a synthesis with other cultures. Genuine renaissance would not be possible without a rediscovery, reaffirmation and renewed commitment with the universals within our culture, that is, the idea of human dignity founded upon spiritual substance, moral well-being and noble sensibility. Human dignity must be promoted in society through justice, virtue and compassion. These transcend cultural and political boundaries. They belong to all, East and West, North and South.

The celebrated humanist of the European Renaissance, Pico della Mirandola wrote:

> We shall live for ever, not in the schools of word-catchers, but in the circle of the wise, where they talk ... of the deeper causes of things human and divine; he who looks closely will see that even the barbarians had intelligence (*mercuriam*), not on the tongue but in the breast.[6]

What it amounts to is that we should pursue our renaissance with the curiosity of a child and the humility of a sage. In this regard, we have to take stock of the experiences of the West. One of the tragedies of that great civilization was the narrowing of its perspective after the outpouring of intellectual and cultural energy fired by the moral release during the Renaissance. With Enlightenment, arrogance began to creep in. Europe no longer wanted to live in the "circle of the wise" but proclaimed that others had to be like them in order to be wise. While Pico had acknowledged the "intelligence" of the barbarians, the Enlightenment philosophers thought only they were the personification of intelligence while the rest were savages fit only to be conquered.

Asians too, in their xenophobic obsession to denounce certain Western ideas as alien, may end up denouncing their own fundamental values and ideals. This is because in the realm of ideas founded upon the humanistic tradition, neither the East nor the West can lay exclusive claim to them. These ideas are universal.

Thus, acceptance that certain ideas are universal, the rejection of cultural jingoism, and taking cognizance of the rich diversity of religions and traditions of mankind are the prerequisites for the flourishing of the Asian Renaissance.

## REBIRTH OF PHILOSOPHY

A renaissance in the realm of philosophy is undoubtedly one of the most productive results of the intellectual encounter between Asia and the West. Iqbal is an example of an Asian creative mind having to grapple with Western philosophical ideas and doctrines which influenced him deeply while expounding the world view of his religion to the West.[7] What Iqbal did for Islam, his contemporary, Sarvepalli Radhakrishnan (1888–1975), did for Hinduism. His writings reveal not only the richness and variety of ancient Indian schools of philosophy but also their relevance to modern times. The significance of Indian philosophy is that it is man's oldest and continuous speculation about the nature of reality and man's place therein. Radhakrishnan stressed the importance of philosophy in the realm of practical affairs. He wrote:

> Social and political conditions in the several areas of the world depend, in the final analysis, upon the philosophical and spiritual thought and ideals of the peoples of the world. The future of civilization depends upon the return of spiritual awareness to the hearts and minds of men.[8]

The search for unity and attempts at synthesis of Asian and Western philosophies continue to preoccupy Asian philosophers of all religious persuasions. In Japan, Nishida Kitaro (1870–1945) founded the Kyoto school of philosophy to embark on civilizational dialogue, principally between East Asian spirituality and the philosophical and religious experience of the West.[9] This served as a catalyst for a new thought movement reflecting the awareness that Asians need to know one another as much as they need to know the West. Japanese scholar and philologist Toshihiko Izutsu (1914–1993) undertook a landmark study of the mystical thoughts of the great Sufi master Ibn Arabi and Taoist philosopher Chuang Tze which led to the discovery of a metaphilosophy of the Oriental philosophies. This dispels the notion that because of its religious diversity, Asia would, *ipso facto*, be culturally divergent and disjointed.[10]

## CULTURAL DIVERSITY

Nations can actually grow and prosper by accepting the fact of cultural diversity, strengthening themselves by learning about their differences as well as by reinforcing the values they share in common. Malaysia is a case in point. It can justifiably claim to be Asia in microcosm – a country with a truly diverse population in terms of ethnicity, culture and faith. Admittedly this has not come about by choice. One might even say that we were forced by circumstances and history to become a nation, not by dissolving our respective identities and loyalties, but by transcending them. Although we still face many challenges to maintain national unity and harmony, we have nevertheless found the situation far more enriching than had we been a predominantly single community.

However, multiculturality can only grow in an open civic culture where the political environment enables full participation and open interaction of all the diverse elements of society. No particular group or sector must be made to feel alienated, deprived or suppressed. We must be open towards institutions, practices and standards which have proven to be efficacious in preventing injustice towards individuals and minorities. This is not an academic issue because virtually all Asian nation states have minorities – ethnic, linguistic and religious. In many cases, the task of nation-building has yet to be completed. Granted, not everyone can proceed towards the future at the same pace; but there is no question of going back to the feudal past.

The upshot of the process of decolonization in Southeast Asia was not only the ejection of the colonial powers, but the empowerment of the people. It liberated their minds and restored their confidence. National independence would not have been possible without the prior cultivation of the spirit of liberty and nurturing of the aspiration for a just social order. Once this took root, it acquired a life of its own. This spirit became the enduring theme in the consolidation period for nation-building, and the great thrust for economic and social upliftment. The recent history of our region has indeed been animated by the quest to provide what is best for the people: the enlargement of liberty, the diffusion of prosperity, justice in the distribution of wealth, and accountability in the public sphere.

## ECONOMIC EMPOWERMENT

The globalization of the Asian economy has proceeded at such a rapid pace that Asian countries will have to break away from narrow nationalistic mindsets and pursue with greater enthusiasm a regional and global agenda. This is a question of necessity and not of choice. Recent events clearly indicate that we are heading towards this direction. The ratification of the General Agreement on Tariffs and Trade (GATT) at the end of 1994 by the major economic powers has sealed the fate of inward-looking policies in favour of freer and more open markets. It remains to be seen whether the operation of the World Trade Organization (WTO) will enhance the economic prospects of individual Asian countries and add confidence, predictability and discipline to the multilateral trading system. The challenge before Asia at this point in time is not simply to grow as an aggregate of separate individual countries, but as a more integrated regional entity. We need to strengthen the building blocks of a regional Asia as a prelude to a global Asia, one which while riding high on the waves of the economic tide, will not lose steam in its current reawakening.

Economic issues cannot be totally separated from social, political, moral and cultural issues that demand the attention of concerned Asians. Economic progress must not be achieved at the expense of social justice. Financial and industrial policies must take into account the needs of the marginalized and disadvantaged groups in our teeming cities as well as in the remote parts of the region. If the rise of Asia is to contribute towards the greater happiness of mankind, then it must not be viewed in confrontational terms, whether economic, political or civilizational. True, wars and conflicts are the very stuff that history is made of, but there can be no greater war than the inner struggle of conscience, the commitment to submit ourselves to commonly shared ideals. Millions of Asians could have been spared their present misery had the societies in which they lived been true to their ideals. Likewise, it will be a betrayal of those ideals if present injustices are perpetuated in the name of adherence to a unique cultural tradition.

The economic empowerment of Asia would not be sustainable unless the new quest for prosperity is inspired by a new social philosophy that is not motivated by pure greed or narrow material pursuit. The new Asia that we envisage will be a lot richer in the broadest sense of the word, if profitability is integrated with social responsibility. Wealth creation is not intended for the enrichment of the few but also to ensure fair and equitable distribution among society at large, for this is the path that will continue to liberate millions from the scourge of poverty and destitution.

Thus, it is imperative that efforts to create a competitively efficient and modern economy be supported and enhanced by ethical business practices that will help to create our own regional ethos, one that emphasizes justice and equity, one that will become the hallmark of an emerging paradigm. We need to evolve a new pattern of relationship, a partnership among people, with our pursuit of wealth matched by our care and compassion for the less fortunate and the disadvantaged. Our drive towards modernization and industrialization must be balanced by a firm belief in positive traditional values and a consciousness to protect the environment. Asians must not repeat the mistakes and excesses of the past inflicted upon them by multinational corporations. In their pursuit of profits, they totally disregarded the adverse long-term impact of their actions on the social fabric and the environment of the host countries.

## STARK CONTRADICTIONS

We must have the courage to address the stark contradictions within our societies. For instance, although we take pride in religiosity continuing to be a major element in our lives, yet, our society seems to be indifferent to the moral decadence and the erosion of the social fabric through widespread permissiveness and corruption. Of course some would say that many of the vices running rampant are but the inevitable consequences of abject poverty. No doubt there is more than a grain of truth in that. Nevertheless, if the practice of religion has been entrenched with its moral and ethical dimensions beyond mere rituals, chants and mantras, then this degeneration would most likely have been kept in check.

27

The euphoria induced by the remarkable economic growth must also not blind us to the parallel rise of corruption: bribery, nepotism and the abuse of power. The argument that this is a necessary evil, using Rostowian stages of growth, and that these excesses are equally prevalent in the West, is self-defeating because vice cannot take the place of virtue whatever may be the ends. This is a fundamental issue which goes to the core of our moral and ethical foundations.

## SELF VERSUS SOCIETY

If the term Asian values is not to ring hollow, Asians must be prepared to champion ideals which are universal. It is altogether shameful, if ingenious, to cite Asian values as an excuse for autocratic practices and denial of basic rights and civil liberties. To say that freedom is Western or unAsian is to offend our own traditions as well as our forefathers who gave their lives in the struggle against tyranny and injustice. It is true that Asians lay great emphasis on order and societal stability. But it is certainly wrong to regard society as a kind of deity upon whose altar the individual must constantly be sacrificed. No Asian tradition can be cited to support the proposition that in Asia, the individual must melt into a faceless community. The Confucian precept which emphasizes discipline and order has often been cited as a rationale for authoritarian rule and the doctrine that the state must always precede the individual. This argument lacks substance. For one, as asserted by Professor Tu Wei-ming, Confucius advocated the primacy of the self, the individual and the community as a *sine qua non* for human flourishing.[11] The Confucian insistence on learning for the sake of the self is predicated on the conviction that self-cultivation is an end in itself rather than a means to an end. Although we are obligated to assume social responsibility and participate in political affairs, it is self-cultivation that would enable us to participate in society and politics as independent moral agents rather than pawns in a game of power relationships. Commenting on Confucius' vision of the relationship between self, family, community, nation and humanity, Huston Smith, an authority on comparative religion studies, noted:

> In shifting the centre of one's concern from oneself to one's family, one transcends selfishness. The move from family to community transcends nepotism. The move from community to nation transcends parochialism, and the move to all humanity counters chauvinistic nationalism.[12]

It has been argued that economic issues must be kept apart from non-economic ones. Neither politics nor morality must disrupt the peaceful clamour of the market-place. This argument is again another gross misrepresentation of what Asian traditions have always stood for. The major Asian traditions stand for a holistic vision of life and society encompassing economic, social and political dimensions as opposed to partialistic and fragmentary approaches to development. If we want to lay claim to a unique Asian way, such a way is none other than the articulation of that vision in unequivocal terms. Central to this vision is the philosophy that economic development must proceed coterminously with cultural enrichment. The pursuit of prosperity must not be at the expense of environmental degradation. The quest for growth must always be balanced by a profound concern for social justice and equity. This is the master key to unlocking the secrets of the Asian Renaissance.

Asia will continue to modernize, even at an accelerated pace, but it does not necessarily mean that it will have to compromise its values and forsake its ideals. However, it needs to be able to give a better account of itself. This discourse might just be the starting point.

No discourse on reengineering, be it on economics or politics, can be fruitful in a climate of intellectual and cultural aridity. The centres of learning and social institutions such as the media should not only be attentive to the real issues affecting society but should actively engage in their discourse. In this regard, intellectual excellence and cultural enrichment must take the place of mediocrity and philistinism. The life of the mind must be cherished and held in high esteem, not forsaken and looked upon with disdain and contempt. Asian governments have often been accused of inhibiting the intelligentsia in their respective jurisdictions from being more openly critical. Perhaps there is some truth in this. But the complaints about the lack of freedom are often exaggerated. The reengineering of society, to make it more open, transparent and tolerant, is also contingent upon a vibrant intellectual climate.

For Asia to be truly global, its societies must be prepared to transform themselves and discard the harmful residue from the past – tribalism, feudalism, narrow-mindedness and fanaticism. It is not the case that Asia must lose its identity, but it must renew commitment to core values such as justice, virtue and compassion, that are in themselves universal. Creativity, imagination and courage is needed to translate these values into reality.

The message of the Asian Renaissance should be heeded not just by the people of this region, but also by our erstwhile colonial masters. It is not enough that they merely express regret and remorse over the treatment meted out to those they once lorded over. Contrition is but the first step towards owning up to past sins. It lacks conviction when old prejudices persist. When they hector us on issues such as human rights, patronize us on the matter of values, impose conditionalities on trade, we cannot help but suspect a hidden agenda – a new form of domination in place of the old. These actions are tantamount to an attempt to frustrate our efforts to build a just and equitable society. The true test, therefore, of their sincerity is whether they would continue to treat us as mere pawns to be manoeuvred according to their dubious designs, or join us as equal partners in actualizing a new moral vision for the world.

Certainly, the task is not a simple one. But its enormity should not lead us to despair. Perhaps the following words from Rabindranath Tagore will serve as a beacon in the hour of darkness:

> In an era of mounting anguish and vanishing worth, when disaster is fast overtaking countries and continents, with savagery let loose and brutal thirst for possession augmented by science, it may sound merely poetic to speak of any emerging principle of worldwide relationship. But Time's violence, however immediately threatening, is circumscribed, and we who live beyond it and dwell also in the larger reality of Time, must renew our faith in the perennial growth of civilization towards an ultimate purpose.[13]

Endnotes

1   Durant, Will, *The Story of Civilization Vol. 5: The Renaissance*, New York: MJF Books, 1953, p. 567.

2   Nasr, Seyyed Hossein, *Religion and the Order of Nature*, New York: Oxford University Press, 1996, Chapter 5.

3   Iqbal, Muhammad, *The Secrets of the Self*, translation and notes by R.A. Nicholson, Lahore: Sh. Muhammad Ashraf, 1972.

4   See Burckhardt, Jacob, *The Civilization of the Renaissance in Italy*, New York: Random House, 1954, p. 4.

5   Rizal, José, Address in Madrid in 1883 titled "Ciencia, Virtud y Trabajo" in *Rizal as an Internationalist*, edited by Regino P. Paular, Manila: National Historical Institute, 1992, p. 59.

6   Quoted by Burckhardt, Jacob, *op. cit.*, p. 147.

7   Iqbal, Muhammad, *The Reconstruction of Religious Thought in Islam*, Lahore: Iqbal Academy of Pakistan, 1958. Like Abraham, he came out of the fire alive, that is, with his Muslim identity intact despite his Western education and his engaging the West in the frontier of philosophy. See An Nadwi, Abul Hasan Ali, *Glory of Iqbal*, translated by Mohammad Asif Kidwai, Lucknow: Academy of Islamic Research and Publications, 1979.

8   Radhakrishnan, Sarvepalli and Moore, Charles A. (eds.), *A Sourcebook in Indian Philosophy*, New Jersey: Princeton University Press, 1957, p. xxxi.

9   Keiji, Nishitani, *Nishida Kitaro*, translated by Yamamoto Keisaku and James W. Heisig, Berkeley: University of California Press, 1983. Japanese philosopher Nishitani Keiji illustrates the internal dynamics of this great cultural rebirth: "... struggling to deepen their own self-awareness and at the same time to understand what it means to be alive ... what was sought was a cultivation of art, history and philosophy that would embrace this world ..."

10  Izutzu, Toshihiko, *Sufism and Taoism*, Berkeley: University of California Press, 1983. See also his essay, "An Analysis of *Wahdat al-Wujud*: Towards a Metaphilosophy of Oriental Philosophies" in *Creation and the Timeless Order of Things*, Ashland: White Cloud Press, 1994.

11  Tu Wei-ming, *Way, Learning and Politics: Essays on the Confucian Intellectual*, Singapore: IEAPE, 1989.

12  Smith, Huston, *The Religions of Man*, New York: Harper and Row, 1986.

13  Tagore, Rabindranath, Address at the Conferment of Doctorate of Letters *Honoris Causa* by Oxford University, 1940, in *Rabindranath Tagore: The Myriad-Minded Man*, by Krishna Dutta and Andrew Robinson, New York: St. Martin's Press, 1995, p. 353.

# Symbiosis Between East and West

In all the literary traditions of mankind, the love story is the most enduring, for love brings forth the best, and also the worst, in man. In *Romeo and Juliet*, Shakespeare rends our hearts with the story of love's entanglement with loyalty. Anguished by the acrimony and bitterness of the family feud, Juliet is prepared to forsake her family for love:

> Deny thy father, and refuse thy name;
> Or, if thou wilt not, be but sworn my love,
> And I'll no longer be a Capulet.[1]

In the encounter between the civilizations of the East and the West, generations of the intelligentsia from the East – the Muslims, the Hindus, the Confucianists – were caught in a predicament profound and far-reaching: whether to remain faithful to one's traditions or to renounce them for a way of life perceived as superior. They generally fell into two distinct categories: those who would forswear everything from the West because of their passionate and tenacious hold on everything from their own traditions; and those who, overawed by the dazzling achievements of Western civilization, had become renegades condemning their own.

Asian history, particularly in the late nineteenth and early twentieth centuries, is replete with instances of rancorous intellectual debate on the attitudes towards Western civilization and the future of traditional cultures. The transformation of Meiji Japan in the second half of the nineteenth century was the earliest and most striking example of Westernization in Asia, illustrating the bitter contest between the two positions. Fukuzawa Yukichi, a leading Meiji educational reformer, stressed the necessity for Japan to acquire not only the external trappings of Western civilization such as the legal and educational systems, as well as its machines and tools, but also to absorb its "internal civilization" such as the moral values, the spirit of learning, the ethos, the customs, the etiquette and other social graces. To him, the inculcation of the internal civilization, being necessarily more complex, took precedence over the outer forms of Western civilization. Along with many others, he believed that comprehensive Westernization was necessary for Japan to achieve parity with Western powers.[2] Another prominent proponent of Westernization, Inoue Kaoru, proposed social programmes not only to bring about greater interaction between Japanese and foreigners, but also to enable Japan to compete with Western powers. He unabashedly declared:

> Let us change our empire into a European-style empire. Let us change our people into a European-style people. Let us create a new European-style empire on the Eastern sea. Only thus can our empire achieve a position equal to that of the Western countries with respect to treaties. Only thus can our empire be independent, prosperous and powerful.[3]

Such a blatant advocacy of Westernization was met with equally fanatical Europhobia among the nationalist-minded elite. The

Confucian tutor to the Meiji Emperor, Motoda Eifu, blamed the Westernized education system for being the source of moral decline and impoverishment of the spirit of the younger generation. Several movements sprang up to champion the cause of native Japanese culture. One of them published a bimonthly, *Nohonjin*, dedicated to "the preservation of the national essence (*kokusui hozon*)." The journal's trenchant criticism of the government's Europeanization policies caused its publication to be suspended several times. It is interesting that four leaders of the movement – Miyake Setsurei, Shiga Shigetaka, Inoe Enryo and Sugiura Jugo – received university education in Western philosophy and science. Sugiura Jugo, who studied chemistry in England and shifted interest to education upon returning to Japan, viewed the education policy of the government as "... a matter of plastering Western civilization on one's person." To him, the basis for Japanese education, or the elements of education necessary for being Japanese, lay in the preservation of the spirit peculiar to the Japanese from ancient times. To cultivate the Japanese spirit among children, one should ensure that they be thoroughly acquainted with the history, literature and culture of their country, and such knowledge was necessary before a student could venture into Western studies.[4]

China, proud and confident for thousands of years, in 1842 was suddenly subject to a system of international relations characterized by "unequal treaties" forced upon it by Western powers. Out of bitterness of defeat, some Chinese intellectuals sought solace in the security of tradition and rejected everything foreign. Others were mesmerized by the wealth and power of the enemy, and saw in the West an image of what Asia should be. The New Culture Movement led by Chien Tu-hsu (1879–1942), for example, denounced Confucianism as an antiquated tradition which caused weakness and collective impotence. They believed Westernization was the only road to regain their lost dignity. Yet there were those who took the middle way by advocating the creation of a "new people" by combining the best elements of East and West. Liang Ch'i-ch'ao, the leader of a reform movement early this century, expressed this position succinctly in 1902:

> The term "new people" does not mean that our people must give up entirely what is old in order to follow others. There are two meanings of "new". One is to temper and grind what is original in the people and so renew it; the other is to adopt what is originally lacking in the people and so make a new people. Without one of the two, there is no success ... Thus, what I mean by "new people" are not those intoxicated with Western custom, despising the morals, academic learning, and customs of our several-thousand-year-old country to keep company with others; nor are they those who stick to old papers and say merely embracing the several thousand years of our own morals, academic learning, and custom will be sufficient to enable us to stand up on the great earth.[5]

The Westernization controversy also sparked intellectual ferment in parts of the world under colonial domination. In the 1930s, when the Egyptian intellectual Dr Taha Husayn asserted that the Egyptian mind was nearer to the Western than the Oriental, and therefore must identify itself with the West, it raised such a storm that the ensuing exchanges reverberated throughout the Muslim world. Almost at the same time, Sutan Takdir Alisjahbana stirred a prolonged debate, known as *Polemik Kebudayaan* (Cultural Polemics), based on his declaration that the West should be the model for modern Indonesia.[6] Indeed one can cite other parallel controversies in many other Asian countries.

## THE MENACING JUGGERNAUT

Today, the theme is still very much alive although it has evolved into more complex alignments reflecting the political changes and intellectual milestones of the last century. A new debate is now brewing, but this time, the exotic, docile and moribund East – "there is too much in Asia and she is too old," according to Kipling – has been transfigured into an energetic and menacing Asia, whose phenomenal economic growth poses a serious challenge to the current dominance of the West vis-à-vis the control and appropriation of the world's vital resources. Asia's cheaply manufactured products are not only a peril to the West's industrial hegemony but also to its sense of well-being. Some even go as far as to portray them as a dire threat to present-day Western lifestyles, and even to Western civilization itself. As the argument goes, the current high standards of living in the West is only possible through a high wage regime. When low wage societies start to flood European and North American markets with their cheap products, such a high wage regime, the very foundation of their leisure and culture, would no longer be sustainable. Thus, the East Asian "miracle" becomes a "nightmare" for the West.

From the time of the Renaissance and through the Enlightenment, the encounter between East and West has been dominated by a particular language of discourse, one which posits reason and enlightenment against superstition and darkness, dynamism and civilization against sterility and barbarism, all part and parcel of the civilizing mission of the West.

True, the age of *la mission civilisatrice* is over and no one talks about it any longer without a touch of remorse or embarrassment. However, in our day, the tone is as condescending, although it has metamorphosed into *la mission démocratisatrice*. That enterprise has acquired the status of a dogma in foreign relations, being espoused with great sophistication, ready to be enforced with the mightiest firepower known in human history.

During the late nineteenth and early twentieth centuries, European writers on Southeast Asia conjured the image of "the lazy native" to justify colonialism.[7] Today, a new image is being distilled in the international mass media and popular travel writings: Asia is an economic juggernaut and the continent a vast sweat shop. It is made up of congested cities and fecund factories, with an endless supply of cheap labour ever ready to be exploited. Fundamental human rights are honoured more in the breach than in the observance. Asian societies are stratified into two levels. On the one hand, there are the downtrodden masses, economically and politically disadvantaged, the plebeians as it were. And on the other hand, lording over the oppressed majority, a patrician class comprising the old aristocracy, the military cliques, and an expanding coterie of equally corrupt opportunists. The perceived excesses and autocratic tendencies of the ruling elites are attributed to Asian values, which, in Western eyes, fall far short of universal ideals.

On the other extreme, Asian spokesmen, in their eagerness to fend off criticism, often indulge in stereotyping the West. Generally, the West is viewed as a morally decadent civilization. In the West, the institution of the family, regarded all over Asia as the very foundation of a civil society, is in ruins. Religion and morality, being matters strictly within the individual domain, have ceased to have any bearing on societal mores. It is said that overindulgence in personal liberties has bred licentiousness to a degree which renders people no different from animals in the pursuit of wanton and depraved lifestyles. In short, the West is seen to be nothing more than a moral wasteland, a lost society of aimless wandering souls.

## FROM PREJUDICES TO PREDILECTIONS

These are complex and difficult issues which require greater mutual understanding and the eradication of deep-rooted suspicions. Prejudices ossified over centuries demand moral commitment and relentless exertion in order to be transformed into predilections. Much of this deep-seated mutual wariness and apprehension are a legacy of colonialism. For instance, the attitudes of Westerners in castigating Asian countries for being sluggish in effecting societal reforms smacks of pure condescension. They should remember that it took the United States almost 100 years to get from the Declaration of Independence to the abolition of slavery; and, after that, almost another 100 years again to arrive at the landmark decision of the Supreme Court in *Brown vs. The Board of Education* in 1954 prohibiting racial segregation in the schools. To allow oneself to be lectured and hectored on freedom and human rights after 100 years of struggle to regain one's liberty and human dignity, by those who had participated in, or benefited from, the subjugation, is to willingly suffer impudence. The present debate about democracy and human rights has therefore been rendered unfruitful because of this inflexibility and semblance of cultural arrogance.

This, however, should not detract from the fact that Asians themselves are guilty of many of the transgressions with which the West has charged them. In many parts of Asia, signs of moral entropy, corruption, nepotism and other excesses abound which the elite, for reasons best known to themselves, choose to gloss over. The recent successes of the economies of Asia, and the growing self-confidence of the people, have on occasions given rise to overtones of arrogance and trumpets of triumphalism. This is a betrayal of one of the most enduring values of the East, that of humility before the vastness of human endeavour and the totality of creation. It is foolhardy to assume that the success of the last thirty years can be repeated over the next thirty. For sustainability, progress in the social and political spheres must be in tandem with economic achievements. Obsession with mere economic indices blinds us to the fact that there remain in our midst considerable pockets of abject poverty and destitution. The pain and misery of exploited labour, including women and children, are very real wherever they occur. Social inequalities, corruption, denial of basic liberties and downright oppression are still rampant. The Asian traditions themselves need to be revitalized and purified from the oppressive, autocratic and feudalistic past. Some are plainly anachronistic, while others do not conform to basic universal norms.

It is against this background that we must engage ourselves in civilizational dialogue, for protracted mutual miscomprehension could lead to a supplanting of the Cold War with more insidious forms of confrontations. Indeed, this dialogue has become imperative at a time when the world has shrunk into a global village, where petty differences could quickly blow up into full-scale conflicts.

This is why the discourse has been transposed from being merely a consideration of cultural differences to a contemplation of an impending clash on a civilizational scale.[8] This is nothing more than Orientalism in new garb, a notion both false and dangerous. It is false because it implies an inherent impermeability of cultures, an inability to absorb each other's characteristics, and presupposes the existence of a "Great Wall" separating the civilizations of the world. It is dangerous because it generates paranoia and breeds animosity and suspicion, and may, therefore, become a self-fulfilling prophecy. Thus, the question is not whether civilizations will clash, but whether civilizations ought to clash.

The dialogue should be continuous and motivated by a genuine search for true understanding. Each party must be prepared to come out of their mental cocoons and transcend the limitations of their thinking. Asia too has still as much to discover about the West, inasmuch as the West has to do more to understand and appreciate Asia. In order to do that, they must break away from the old mindset and should not, to paraphrase T.S. Eliot, revive old factions, restore old policies or follow an antique drum.[9]

If we transcend the noise of the day, and reflect more on higher ideals, we will discover that there is less difference between East and West than is often made out to be. There is no basis for doubting that the West is any less dedicated to ethical and moral ideals or to the virtues of family life than the East. The challenge at hand is to conceive a common vision of the future which goes beyond our current concerns and preoccupations, advancing towards the creation of a global community, dominated neither by the East nor the West, but dedicated to the ideals of both.

It is significant that the Quranic injunction, expressed as *li ta'ārafū* – to get to know one another – is addressed to mankind as a whole, not to Muslims alone.

> Oh mankind, we created you from a single pair of a male and a female, and made you into nations and tribes that you may know one another. Verily, the most honoured of you in the sight of God is the most righteous of you. And God has full knowledge and is well acquainted with all things.[10]

## CONSENSUS AD IDEM

We are already in fundamental agreement, in that we subscribe to the universal quest for truth and the pursuit of justice and virtue. We rejoice in beauty, both within ourselves and in what surrounds us. We long for knowledge, peace and security amid the mysteries and uncertainties of the universe. In our disjointed world, therefore, with so much ugliness, violence and injustice, there cannot be a nobler aim and vocation than the realization of values which unify humanity, despite the great diversity of climes and cultures.

In *Choruses from 'The Rock'*, T.S. Eliot laments thus:

All our knowledge brings us nearer to our ignorance,
All our ignorance brings us nearer to death,
But nearness to death no nearer to GOD.
Where is the Life we have lost in living?
Where is the wisdom we have lost in knowledge?
Where is the knowledge we have lost in information?[11]

The poignancy of the questions is even more profoundly felt today than when they were first raised. Perhaps the experience of the Muslims is a good case in point. No community has suffered more wrong from the information explosion than they have. The gullible consumer of the mass media of today would form the impression that the Muslim world is only populated by stern and menacing fundamentalists. Isolated incidents of violence and terrorism perpetrated by groups waving the fundamentalist or *jihad* banner will invariably stir up mass hysteria against Muslims. The fact of the matter is, a majority of Muslims in this present day are themselves living in poverty or under tyrannical regimes. We are deeply aware that the Muslim world is not without its excesses and internal contradictions. The negative image of Muslims to the rest of the world is to a certain extent the result of the failure of many Muslims themselves to realize and manifest their own ideals.

Notwithstanding this, the Muslim is not without a sense of humour, and his civilization has produced plenty of love stories. For example, from the Moroccan coast of the Atlantic to the tiny Merauke island of Indonesia in the Pacific, Muslim children are raised with the enchanting tale of love between Laila and Majnun. As the story goes, the young man was scorned and ridiculed for his obsession with the maiden, because to the eyes of the world Laila was hideous in physical appearance. In response to this, the youth always replied: "To see the beauty of Laila, one requires the eyes of Majnun."

## CONSORTIUM OF CULTURES

As Asia renews itself, it must have the confidence to appreciate and learn from Western civilization, inasmuch as the West has to learn from the East. If the dialogue between Asian and Western civilizations is to become truly fruitful, Asians must transcend the pain and bitterness following their earlier encounters, while the West needs to adopt other languages of discourse apart from the one presented since the Renaissance and the Enlightenment. The East must look beyond the Crusades and the era of colonialism, while the West must look at the East and the rest of the world in a new light, a perspective illuminated by humility and sincerity.

The supreme Christian poet, Dante Alighieri, in the twelfth century, envisaged the establishment of the "universal community of the human race", a community dedicated to justice and the realization of man's intellectual potential. Although Dante's propositions would appear to be rather mild and commonplace in this day and age, nevertheless, such a concept stood in stark contrast to the notion of universal Christendom prevalent in his time. What he propounded was radical and revolutionary.

Even more significant is the fact that it was not from the writings of the doctors of the Church that Dante formulated his political philosophy, but from the ruminations of Averroes (Ibn Rushd) on the doctrine of the Universal Intellect. By transposing Averroes' doctrine, which was essentially metaphysical in purport, onto the plane of the human community, Dante expounded the idea of the unity of the human race. That single community of man must be established first in order to secure universal peace. According to Dante:

> Since, therefore, the matter under discussion is political, or rather the source and principle of all correct politics, and since everything political is subject to our power, it is evident that the matter under discussion is not concerned in the first place with speculation, but with action.[12]

Dante's idea of the "universal community of the human race" was in fact realized for centuries in Spain under Moorish rule. This period, known as the *convivencia*, witnessed the generally peaceful coexistence between the Jews, Christians and Muslims, where there was fertile cross-pollination of ideas and knowledge dominated by a climate of cultural vitality. Christians built their homes in the Moorish style and dressed in Arab clothing. Jewish and Muslim literature was translated into Castillian and Latin. Notwithstanding the Christian reconquest in the eleventh and twelfth centuries, Muslim populations continued to grow in Toledo and Zaragosa. Even as James I of Aragon endeavoured to establish Christian hegemony by bringing in new settlers and setting up new orders, the Christians generally left the Muslims alone to carry on with their lives and daily activities. Muslim merchants and artisans continued to prosper.[13]

Averroes' commentaries on Aristotle and the works of Maimonides were translated into Latin and quoted by St. Thomas Aquinas. It was from the Spanish Arab scholars and their disciples like Roger Bacon, Michael Scott and Peter Abelard, that Europe received "the spirit which has enabled man to dominate the world and utilize it to his own ends."[14]

## ENGAGEMENT WITH THE WEST

The primary motif of civilizational dialogue must be a global *convivencia*, a harmonious and enriching experience of living together among people of diverse religions and cultures. To enter a more meaningful stage of engagement between Asia and the West, it must be an encounter between equals, between cherished ideals and values that will serve to challenge our pride and end our prejudices. In the domain of trade and economics, it is quite clear that the West looks at Asia as a force to be reckoned with. Equally clear, however, is a reluctance to accord a similar recognition to Asia's cultural and civilizational aspirations. Prosperity is a confidence booster. And this renewed self-esteem has spawned a growing desire among Asians to share the burden of reshaping the world, rather than being shaped by others as was the case in the past. The economic rise of Asia should therefore lead to greater interdependence and genuine mutual consultation in the years to come.

The perception of the West toward Asia has changed little over the centuries – as *terra incognita* in the fifteenth century, as the yellow peril during the Cold War and finally in our time as intimidating dragons and tigers. It is an irony that as the world becomes smaller, the consciousness of the division and divide among the human community magnifies: the East and the West, the North and the South, the powerful and the marginalized. Much of this division has come about and is perpetuated by the practice of polity that has become totally identified with the exercise of power, and leadership that is increasingly divorced from ethical concerns and morality. Enduring peace and security of the world must be built not upon religious, cultural, economic or political hegemonies but on mutual awareness and concern. For understanding brings respect, and respect prepares the way for love. Love, like truth, liberates and takes us on to a higher kind of loyalty, onto what is true, just and virtuous.

## Endnotes

1   Shakespeare, *Romeo and Juliet*, Act II, scene ii.

2   Tsunoda, R. Yusaku, de Bary, Wm Theodore and Keene, Donald, *Sources of Japanese Tradition Vol. 2*, New York: Columbia University Press, 1964, pp. 116–130.

3   *Ibid.*

4   *Ibid.*

5   Teng, Ssu-yu, and Fairbank, John K., *China's Response to the West: A Documentary Survey, 1839–1923*, Cambridge: Harvard University Press, 1982, pp. 222–223.

6   Alisjahbana, Sutan Takdir, *Polemik Kebudayaan*, Jakarta: PT Dunia Pustaka Jaya, 1950, p. 42. "... the Indonesian mind must be taught to equal the Western mind."

7   Alatas, Syed Hussein, *The Myth of the Lazy Native*, London: Frank Cass and Co. Ltd, 1977.

8   Huntington, Samuel P., *The Clash of Civilizations and the Remaking of World Order*, New York: Simon and Schuster, 1996.

9   Eliot, T.S., *Four Quartets: Little Gidding*, New York: Harvest Books, 1971.

10  *al-Ḥujarāt* 49:13.

11  Eliot, T.S., *Selected Poems*, New York: Harvest Books, 1964.

12  Dante Alighieri, *Monarchy*, cited by Etienne Gilson in *Dante and Philosophy*, translated by David Moore, New York: Harper and Row, 1963, p. 171.

13  Lapidus, Ira M., *A History of Islamic Societies*, Cambridge: Cambridge University Press, 1988, p. 388.

14  Irving, T.B., *Falcon of Spain*, Lahore: Sh. Muhammad Ashraf, 1973, p. 144.

# Democracy and Civil Society

Little noticed by much of the West, Asia is witnessing the revival of the debate over democracy and civil society. This discourse, rooted in Asian traditions and culture, is led by a new generation of confident and assertive Asians – intellectuals, social activists, artists and politicians – who subscribe to the universality of democratic values.

The debate is in part fuelled by a new sense of confidence acquired following a period of sustained economic growth and political stability. The impact is greater than that of the process of decolonization some five decades ago, reshaping the global order and propelling Asia to the centre of world affairs.

At the same time, Asian societies are undergoing internal transformations. The soul of Asia is being reconstituted. The integration of Asia with global systems and the interaction between its cultures and that of the West have permanently altered its character.

The on-going discourse on democracy and civil society is also influenced by the peculiar norms and mores of Asian cultures. In short, as Alexis de Tocqueville wrote, it is a debate shaped by the "customs" – the whole moral and intellectual condition, including the "habits of the heart" – of people whose religious, cultural and ethnic diversity far surpasses that found in any other part of the world.[1]

The outcome of these exchanges is a less dogmatic, much richer and more pluralistic conception of democracy and civil society. The diverse possibilities of democracy, shaped by differing laws and mores, were also alluded to by Tocqueville. He wrote:

> ... the Americans have shown that it would be wrong to despair of regulating democracy by the aid of customs and laws. If other nations should borrow this general and pregnant idea from the Americans, without, however, intending to imitate them in the peculiar application which they have made of it ... what reason is there to suppose their efforts would not be crowned with success?[2]

The consensus in Asia is that for civil society to thrive, there must be a strong and vibrant economy, which in turn is predicated upon a stable social and political order. While it is true that freedom and democracy have their intrinsic values and their basic principles must be understood and cherished, priorities must be put right. East Asia could not have achieved such impressive economic results without stability. The urgency accorded by Asians to economic development is understandable. Poverty and the inequitable distribution of economic opportunities are sources of a host of social evils. They breed discontent, frustration and anger, and can destroy the very fabric of society. Thus, freedom and democracy would be seriously compromised if prescribed without due consideration to economic progress and the maintenance of a stable socio-political order.

Now that Asia is secure in its economic stability and vibrancy, it is embarking on a venture to reinvent its social and political order.

The present quest for democracy and civil society is an integral part of the continuum of the movement for national liberation and self-determination which began in the first half of the century.

In this renewed search, Asia has dusted off the shelves the ideals and values expounded by its ancient philosophers and championed by the early figures of the Asian Renaissance: poets, thinkers and statesmen such as Rabindranath Tagore, Muhammad Iqbal, José Rizal, Sun Yat-sen and Mahatma Gandhi. They demonstrated that Asia and Asian traditions are part and parcel of a world built on the dignity of man, an ideal which in the recent past had been purportedly the exclusive domain of the West.

## DIGNITY OF MAN

The creation of a civil society in Asia will no doubt be a gradual process and the path is fraught with challenges. We must remain focused on its basic needs. Foremost is the creation and preservation of social order, without which there will be chaos. Freedom, under the circumstances, will be illusory. In a truly democratic regime, such an order is to be achieved through the exercise of authority with accountability, not merely by the coercive power of the state. On the part of the people, the proper and legitimate assertion of one's individual rights must go hand in hand with the recognition of private duties towards the public good. Liberty must not be allowed to degenerate into immorality and permissiveness. This sense of social discipline must exist if we are to bring to fruition a civil society built upon our ideals of democracy.

The basic proposition governing democracy and civil society is the idea of the dignity of man. That idea took a long time to grow. The earliest comprehensive formulation of the concept of the dignity of man in the West was made during the Renaissance by Pico della Mirandola in an oration delivered to an audience of priests:

I have read, reverend Fathers, in the works of the Arabs, that when Abdala the Saracen was asked what he regarded as most to be wondered at on the world's stage, so to speak, he answered that there is nothing to be seen more wonderful than man (*nihil spectari homine admirabilius*).[3]

This Abdala the Saracen, the source of Pico's idea on the dignity of man, could be no other person than Ibn Qutaiba, the celebrated humanist of the Abbasid era and author of *Khalq al-Insān* or *The Creation of Man*.

A century and a half after Pico, the idea of the dignity of man was to be expressed in unsurpassed beauty and brevity in Shakespeare's *Hamlet*:

What a piece of work is a man! How noble in reason! how infinite in faculty! in form, in moving, how express and admirable! in action how like an angel! in apprehension how like a god! the beauty of the world! the paragon of animals![4]

Democracy should not be an end unto itself, but merely the means by which we can ensure humane governance: the restoring of the dignity of the human person and satisfying the hunger for justice. There can be no dignity in poverty, sickness, deprivation, illiteracy and ignorance. Nor can there be dignity when women continue to be denied equal status, opportunities and remuneration. There can be no justice when the individual is oppressed and fundamental rights are denied him and when whole populations are trapped in war and senseless slaughter. We are nowhere near dignity or justice when the global order is dominated by a few who preach democracy at home and blatantly deny it abroad, when 85 percent of the world's wealth is enjoyed by 20 percent of the global population. Our ultimate goal must be nothing less than the establishment of a just and equitable society.

The civil society we envisage is one based on moral principles, where governance is by rule of law not human caprice, where the growth of civic organizations is nurtured not suppressed, where dissent is not stifled, and where the pursuit of excellence and the cultivation of good taste takes the place of mediocrity and philistinism. For that, we have to retrieve, revive and reinvigorate the spirit of liberty, individualism, humanism and tolerance.

The fact that Asian countries are in different stages of economic development suggests that each country will negotiate its way to democracy and civil society at its own pace. This is further attenuated by the diversity of cultures, social systems and historical experiences. While accepting that all humanitarian ideals are universal, we cannot deny that cultural diversity exerts a powerful influence on the social and political processes.

Consequently, the Asian vision of civil society departs in a fundamental respect from that articulated by some Western thinkers, which is derived mainly from the social philosophy of the Enlightenment. The basic doctrine of this philosophy is that religion and civil society are intrinsically incompatible. Asians would find greater affinity with the precepts of the Founding Fathers of America in marrying civic republicanism with the Puritan religious heritage. This is because religion and spirituality run deep in the Asian psyche. Religion has been a source of great strength to Asian society and will continue to be a bulwark against moral and social decay.

More fundamentally, the Asian world view and its intellectual resources will shape its civil society in its own direction. Foremost among them is the concept of man as a moral being with a transcendent dimension, endowed not only with inalienable rights but also with unshirkable responsibilities: to God, to family, to fellow humans and to nature.

## LIFE'S INVIOLABILITY

For humane governance, it is essential that power be vested in a democratically constituted authority rather than in the hands of an individual. Power personalized is power plundered from the people. Democracy is not a luxury that Asians cannot afford, as some would have us believe. On the contrary, it is a basic necessity for responsible and ethical governance. As Reinhold Niebuhr said: "Man's capacity for justice makes democracy possible, but man's inclination to injustice makes democracy necessary."[5]

Properly instituted, democracy will ensure order and stability. Because it allows for legitimate grievances to be aired and contentious issues to be openly debated, democracy prevents the accumulation of violent and disruptive forces.

The pursuit of economic prosperity is no justification for the persistent and flagrant deprivation of political and civil liberties. In fact, increasing wealth should be the occasion for the extension of freedoms to all spheres, these being the legitimate expectations of a civil society. Notwithstanding the moral basis envisaged in our concept of civil society, these include the expectations that certain fundamental liberties and rights are inviolable and cannot be taken away without due process of law. The Prophet of Islam in his *Hajja al-Widāᶜ* (*Farewell Pilgrimage*) said: "O Mankind, your blood, your property and your honour are as sacred as this Holy Land."[6]

This doctrine of inviolability of man cuts across civilizations. When John Locke launched a revolution in political thought in the seventeenth century to emancipate man from political tyranny, central to his thesis was the idea of the inviolability of human life and property:

Every man is born with a double right. First, a right of freedom to his person which no other man has a power over, but the free disposal of it lies in himself. Secondly, a right before any other man, to inherit, with his brethren, his father's goods.[7]

In resisting democratization, some would argue that the people are not sophisticated enough to practise democracy. To this, Dr Sun Yat-sen replied earlier this century, "Alas! This is like telling a child that he cannot go to school because he is illiterate."[8]

This does not mean that democracy should be unfettered. For democracy without restraints will lead to chaos. Unbridled individualism cannot but paralyse our predisposition for consensus in nation-building. The answer lies in treading the middle path between anarchy and absolutism.

In the multicultural, multi-religious, and multi-ethnic context that we live in, this approach takes on added significance. Each community will always have its extremist fringe, which if given free rein would whip up sentiments to plunge entire nations into turmoil and even bloodshed. It is crucial that we have a moderate majority, one that will be prepared to act firmly and decisively against extremist elements. Lest we forget, democracy itself can only flourish in a nation at peace, where there is mutual tolerance and respect between communities and ethnic groups. In Vaclav Havel's words:

> ... we are witness to a bizarre state of affairs: society had freed itself, true, but in some ways it behaves worse then when it was in chains. Criminality has grown rapidly, and the familiar sewage that in times of historical reversal always wells up from the nether regions of the collective psyche has overflowed into the mass media, especially the gutter press. But there are other, more serious and dangerous symptoms: hatred among nationalities, suspicion, racism, even signs of fascism; intrigue, and deliberate

lying; politicking, an unrestrained, unheedful struggle for purely private interests, a hunger for power, unadulterated ambition, fanaticism of every imaginable kind; new and unprecedented varieties of robbery, the rise of different mafias; the general lack of tolerance, understanding, taste, moderation, reason.[9]

The fact that democracy is often abused, leading to chaos and paralysis, does not mean that dictatorship is the answer. Rather, the solution lies in purging democracy of its excesses such as unrestrained individualism on the one hand, and mob rule on the other. Thus, democracy must be revitalized by infusing it with ethical principles and moral uprightness derived from Asian civilizational ideals and intellectual legacies.

## THE PRESS IN ASIA

The press in Asia is perhaps most influential in setting the agenda for progress toward democracy and the establishment of a civil society. This influence, if anything, has become even more enhanced with the advent of the Information Age. Asian societies in particular are at a stage of development where they are in great need of a dynamic and vibrant press to provide the necessary impetus for progress and to ensure that those in power do not betray the legitimate expectations of the people. One of the greatest challenges facing Asia is the struggle to eradicate the vestiges of so-called "Oriental despotism". They will remain unless Asians vigorously develop and enhance the workings of truly representative participatory governments, promote the rule of law, and foster the cultivation of a free and responsible press. The media is often viewed with great trepidation by those in authority, whether in the East or the West, because of the awesome power it possesses. Napoléon Bonaparte was reported to have said: "Four hostile newspapers are more to be feared than a thousand bayonets."

The mass media in Asia are in fact inheritors of a tradition of journalism which has always been at the forefront of Asia's quest for freedom and progress. Pioneers of Asian journalism included earlier reformers and nationalists who were at the same time littérateurs. They published journals, pamphlets, novels and short stories as vehicles to rouse society from its centuries of slumber and inertia to agitate against colonialism. Like their counterparts in the West, they too had to struggle with the powers that be. If in the West they had to fight against the absolutism of monarchies, Asians had to resist the combined power of feudalism and colonialism. There is, therefore, no basis to dichotomize journalism into Asian and Western, as if the two are distinct and diametrically opposed. The pursuit of freedom and justice is not the sole prerogative of the Western press as Asian history bears testimony to no less heroic struggles by Asian journalists in defence of these ideals. The founding of a journal such as *al-ʿUrwa al-Wuthqā* by Jamaluddin al-Afghani in the later part of the nineteenth century marked a critical juncture in unifying the anti-colonial struggles of a vast number of people in Asia and Africa; the journal *Sin Ch'ao (New Tide)* propelled the May 4th Movement in China earlier this century; at about the same time, in colonial Indonesia, the magazine *Pujangga Baru* provided the intellectual and cultural foundation for the ensuing war of independence; in Malaya, *al-Imām* fostered a sense of national consciousness among the Malay population; and decades before all these, there already were, in India, several influential publications such as *Kesari (Lion)*, the *Bengali* and *Indu Prakash*, all literary thorns in the British side.

Historically, Asian journals and newspapers have been sparks which ignited the flames of anti-colonialism. In the post-independence era, they have been preoccupied with the all-encompassing task of nation-building. By and large, they have succeeded. However, in facing the new realities of Asia, the media in Asian societies have to redefine their role. The press in Asia have to find a middle ground between unconstrained freedom and fawning subservience.

The usual contention is that since freedom cannot be absolute, the press must be restricted. This argument is fallacious, because the concept of press freedom already implies the freedom to speak the truth and not to spread falsehood or undermine public security and corrupt public morals. In any society or country, there are laws on pornography, blasphemy, defamation, conspiracy to cause public disturbance, and so on. In addition, the press is bound by the norms of morality and good taste appropriate to the society in which it operates. Subject to these constraints imposed by virtue of common sense, there is really no case for denying press freedom. Those who contend that press freedom is a luxury for developing countries, their societies being too fragile and not ready for the dissent and conflict generated by a free press, ignore 200 years of Asian history.

In some developing countries, however, the media's complaints about being muzzled and gagged are more often than not the result of their own imaginings. It is instructive that the thoughts and ideas that have survived and withstood the test of time were expressed by courageous people who risked their lives in times when speech was dangerous and censorship was the rule rather than the exception. Yet, in our own day, in spite of the vast opportunities for journalists to exercise their freedom, many have chosen to emasculate themselves and serve as eunuchs of the rich and powerful. Hence, the more fruitful debate is not so much about freedom from censorship, but rather about the need to break loose from the yoke of self-imposed obsequiousness. The media need to emerge as the podium for the encounter of ideas and opinions, as well as the catalyst for the emancipation of the mind from servitude and servility.

The challenge to press freedom does not, of course, come entirely from those holding political power. Those holding economic power may and do subject the press to the dictates of their own personal ambitions and self-centred interests. The agendas and priorities of the media barons are not necessarily predicated upon the interest of the general public. It is incumbent on professional journalists themselves to have the moral courage and conviction to resist the manipulation of the media by vested and selfish interests who have no regard for truth, fairness or the common good. Press freedom should not be used to give free rein to the venting of sectarian sentiments, the manipulation of racial prejudices and religious bigotry, and the fabrication of lies.

The model envisaged is that of a free press that is committed to societal ideals and the enduring values of Asian traditions. Freedom without commitment will strip the press of its sense of direction. The Western press is certainly free, but it has been drifting aimlessly for want of such a commitment, which also reflects the state of its own society. Rather than thriving on sensationalism, acrimony, mud-slinging and stirring up animosities, the press in Asia should seek to harness societal energies towards the realization of cherished ideals: justice, virtue and compassion.

## TIME OF PARADOX

We live in a time of paradox. Autocratic regimes are increasingly under siege, and democracy in its various forms has reached more of the globe than ever before in history. And yet, there is a growing cynicism about democracy and politics in general, due to the inherent contradictions and weaknesses of the system. Faith in the institutions of civil society is being shaken to its roots.

The truth is, despite many millennia of human existence and struggle, the human condition leaves much to be desired. And the burden, as usual, falls most on those least able to bear it, the destitute and the weak. Many a time, the cry of humanity has moved the world to make amends. Sometimes, we have succeeded. But often, we have failed. We have been weak in resolve, inadequate in effort, unwilling of service and sacrifice, and too preoccupied with our own narrow interests.

This is a clear indictment of the failure of our elites. The hallmark of leadership, among other things, is to act on conviction based on principles, rather than to pander to the whims and fancies of the mob, as measured by public opinion polls. Much too often these days the leitmotif of leadership is to do what is politically expedient rather than morally right. At the other extreme, of course, are those who rule by fiat, forgetting that dissent is also a true barometer of the democracy that we claim to uphold. A case can be easily made, not for mere tolerance, but rather for the active nurturing of alternative views. This would necessarily include lending a receptive ear to the voices of the politically oppressed, the socially marginalized and the economically disadvantaged. Ultimately, the legitimacy of a leadership rests as much on moral uprightness as it does on popular support. Democracy should never be allowed to become a concert for the rich and the powerful, for that will mean that we have merely exchanged the rule of the zamindars, encomenderos and feudal lords for the dictatorship of corporate czars, military juntas and political apparatchiks.

The test of true democracy lies in the extent of the people's participation in the democratic process and overall societal development. Thus, it is incumbent upon all of us to nurture the advancement of a civil society. This is the process of conscientization

– making citizens aware of their fundamental rights and encouraging them to act diligently to safeguard their basic liberties from being eroded or trampled upon. They should not suffer in silence while injustices are perpetrated in their midst. This process is crucial to ensure the protection of the development of civil society.

A revolution in consciousness, a reorganization of our collective memory and a change in our self-image is the *sine qua non* for renewal and renovation. As Apolinario Mabini, a luminary of the Philippine Revolution, puts it:

> In order to build the proper edifice of our social generation, it is imperative that we change radically not only our institutions but also our manner of behaving and thinking. It is necessary to have both an external and internal revolution, by establishing our moral education on a more solid foundation and purging ourselves of ... vices.[10]

Endnotes

1   Tocqueville, Alexis de, *Democracy in America*, New York: Alfred A. Knopf, 1963, Vol. 1, p. 299.

2   *Ibid*, p. 325.

3   Cassirer, Ernst, *Renaissance Philosophy of Man*, Chicago: University of Chicago Press, 1956.

4   Shakespeare, *Hamlet*, Act II, scene ii.

5   Niebuhr, Reinhold, *The Children of Light and the Children of Darkness*, New York: Charles Scribner's Sons, 1960.

6   Hadith narrated by Bukhari.

7   Locke, John, "An Essay Concerning the True Original Extent and End of Civil Government" in *Great Books of the Western World Vol. 33*, edited by Mortimer J. Adler, Chicago: Encyclopaedia Britannica, Inc., 1991, p. 69.

8   Sun Yat-sen, "The Three Principles of the People" in *Prescriptions for Saving China: Selected Writings by Sun Yat-sen*, edited by Julie Lee Wei, *et al.*, California: Hoover Institution Press, 1994, p. 228.

9   Havel, Vaclav, "Paradise Lost" in the *New York Review of Books*, April 9, 1992.

10  Majul, Cesar Adib, *Mabini*, Quezon City: Diliman, 1960, p. 128.

# Justice and the Law

When men form a compact to establish a civil society or a political community, they are in need of an organizing principle without which the community will disintegrate. This principle is none other than justice. As Aristotle said: "Justice is the bond of men in states, for the administration of justice, which is the determination of what is just, is the principle of order in a political community."

The principle of justice is so central in a civil society that without it, the concept of law has no meaning. St. Augustine said that "there is no law unless it be just" and that kingdoms are but great robberies if justice is taken away.[1] For Thomas Aquinas, "the force of law depends on the extent of its justice."[2] Alexis de Tocqueville wrote: "There is one universal law that has been formed by the majority of mankind. That law is justice. Justice forms the cornerstone of each nation's law."[3]

The Quran enjoins as follows: "Whenever you judge between people, judge with justice."[4] In the same vein, Muslim philosopher al-Farabi designates justice as a principal attribute of the leader and the people inhabiting the Virtuous City.

So integral is the idea of justice to man that no society is devoid of its conception, and each has evolved its own institution to embody it. Whole societies have been stirred into action in the pursuit of justice and good governance, overthrowing colonial powers and foreign oppressors. Unfortunately, having gained their independence, some countries, while making rapid strides in economic and social development, have not achieved a comparable progress in building the institutions of civil society, particularly the realm of justice and good governance. It would be a tragedy indeed if this hard-earned freedom were to result merely in the substitution of a foreign oppressor with a domestic one, or as in George Orwell's *Animal Farm*, the replacement of the two-legged animal by the four-legged.

It is a legitimate expectation of the citizenry that they be governed with justice by those entrusted with power and authority. The holders of public office therefore carry a sacred trust from all those who had given their lives and property in the struggles for independence of our nations. To be conscientious of the people's expectations as regards justice, accountability and good governance, we must look upon power and authority not as right and privilege, but as duty and obligation.

The issue of justice and governance also concerns the moral responsibility and integrity of those who hold public office. Since laws can be made and unmade by those who control the legislature, law-makers must be imbued with a sense of integrity and motivated not by self-interest but by considerations *pro bono publico*. For Thomas Aquinas, laws were just when they served the common good, distributed burdens fairly, promoted religion, and were within the bounds of the law-maker's authority.[5]

# THE RULE OF LAW

In as much as there is no law without justice, there is no justice without the rule of law. This concept encapsulates three principles. The first is the predominance of regular law so that the government has no arbitrary authority over the citizen. Secondly, all citizens are equally subject to the ordinary law administered by the ordinary courts. And thirdly, perhaps the most significant, the citizen's personal freedoms are formulated and protected by the ordinary law, rather than by abstract constitutional declarations.

The rule of law is the use of law to curb the misuse or abuse of law-making power by the authorities. Law-makers must fulfil their duty to pass only laws that meet the criterion of justness. For if the laws passed by the legislature are manifestly unjust even to the man in the street, then that would put the rule of law in jeopardy.

One of the hallmarks of a civil society is the creation of entrenched constitutional safeguards for the protection of the people's civil rights and liberties. This is an area which demands an innovative and creative approach, fortified by a sense of moral conviction on the part of legislators. In the pursuit of this, there must always be a sense of balance between upholding the rights of the individual and maintaining public order and security.

Man has a dual nature; he is both his own person and a member of his community. On the one hand, the law must protect the individual from the injustices of the multitude. History has shown how individuals fall prey to mass perversity, their crime being simply a refusal to conform to the beliefs and prejudices of the majority. The religious wars in Europe left such a scar in the psyche of the West that the protection of the conscience of the individual has taken priority over all else.

On the other hand, society, being an entity established for the civilized conduct of human affairs, has fundamental rights which are essential for its continued existence. These are rights to maintain law and order, peace and harmony. In this regard, society has the right to defend itself against diabolical minds which see in guarantees of civil liberties opportunities to pursue their vile designs to the detriment of the public. In established democracies, certain individuals use the cloak of individual rights to vent their base desires at the expense of the rights of the majority.

The maintenance of the rule of law hinges on the clear separation of powers between the three branches of government – the legislature, the executive and the judiciary. Inasmuch as parliamentarians are not expected to adjudicate on the laws of a community or country, judges should not take it upon themselves to act as parliamentary draughtsmen or apologists for the executive. As a restraint on the temptation to abuse or misuse power, it is crucial that legal systems be adequately equipped with the necessary checks and balances.

Judges ought to exercise their judicial powers in accordance with the rule of law and not the rule of men. In so doing, judges must constantly bear in mind the legitimate expectations of the people as to their competency, dedication and impartiality. An independent judiciary is a judiciary committed to the preservation of the rule of law. We do not advocate that such a judiciary, in order to be effective, must necessarily take on an anti-establishment posture. But it must, at the very least, be seen to be able to dispense justice without regard to wealth, power or status. As Socrates said: "Four things belong to a judge: to hear courteously, to answer wisely, to consider soberly, and to decide impartially." The growing concern of the public regarding the increasing incidences of judicial indiscretions is a matter to be neither taken lightly nor viewed negatively.

In tandem with the growing maturity of our society, the people's consciousness and expectations of the moral dimension of justice is greater. Not only must judges display the requisite level of competence and expertise, they must, like Caesar's wife, be above suspicion. Thus, judges must be seen to be absolutely impartial in the adjudication of all cases, be they commercial, civil, criminal or constitutional.

In the case of East Asia, this is essential to bolster the region's image as a place where justice can be readily sought and obtained. This is particularly relevant in an era of deregulation and the explosion of the free market when corporations are steadily encroaching into the spheres of society once considered the preserve of governments. Corporations, with their eyes constantly on the bottom line, are not known to be coy about exercising their power to influence judgments in their favour. In seeking legal redress, the poor and the weak are, in some cases, cowed into submission by the rich and the powerful who are armed to the hilt with the most sophisticated legal weaponry and judicial firepower. Under such circumstances, justice can be elusive if not altogether impossible.

In this regard, of paramount importance will be the promotion of social justice via the legal and judicial apparatus to ensure that no group will be unduly marginalized. This apparatus must not be limited to mere legal aid to help those who cannot afford legal redress but must extend to proactive assistance to further the cause of justice through the legal process, without fear or favour.

Among contemporary thinkers, John Rawls is probably the most persuasive in expounding the doctrine that justice is the criterion of the worthiness of social institutions. According to him, laws and institutions, no matter how efficient and well-arranged, must be reformed or abolished if they are unjust. Thus, every individual possesses rights founded on justice which are inviolable.[6]

In regard to the pronouncements and decisions of our judges, it is pertinent to remember what Justice Oliver Wendell Holmes said almost 100 years ago: "The law is the witness and external deposit of our moral life. Its history is the history of the moral development of the race."[7] It is, therefore, vital that we leave behind a legacy of just laws if we are to be remembered as being instrumental in building a dynamic and progressive judicial landscape.

Thus, the challenge is not only to ensure that all our laws are manifestly just but also that they be administered justly without regard to a person's wealth or standing in society. There is nothing more tragic than just laws being administered unjustly. It is dangerous to allow the law to be thought of as something quite distinct from justice in the moral sense, or else it would be possible to blatantly commit injustices by purportedly lawful means. Our courts of law must, at the same time, be courts of justice. Their judgments must conform not only to strict legal requirements but also to the dictates of fairness and equity. If those judgments seek merely to pander to the needs of legal sophistry at the expense of common sense and fair play, then they are perverse. Thus, in a critique of the American legal system, Philip K. Howard wrote:

> Modern law is a game of parsing and logical intrigue. Wherever detailed provisions bend and twist, the observant lawyer will find a place where he can go and violate the spirit of the rules, or get an advantage over others, and do so with complete impunity.[8]

## THE ROLE OF LAWYERS

Given the rapid developments around us, it would not be misplaced to attempt a reappraisal of the role of lawyers as our societies become more advanced and sophisticated. The popular image of lawyers is not flattering. Though the reputation is largely undeserved, it is nevertheless part of the popular imagination all over the world. A Japanese proverb, for example, says that "only painters and lawyers can change white to black." According to an English saying, "There are only two kinds of lawyers, those who know the law and those who know the judge." Notwithstanding this, in general, the legal profession comprises conscientious professionals who practise law true to their calling. And it is to them that the question of their roles in our rapidly changing societies need to be addressed.

To begin with, lawyers must maintain the highest standards of competency and professional ethics. They should also do more public service and make legal expertise more accessible to the less affluent. The law must also be demystified. Lawyers must not, consciously or unconsciously, with intent or otherwise, seek or cause to obfuscate the minds of the people with legal gobbledegook.

The rapid economic and material progress being experienced by the countries in East Asia will significantly impact on the geopolitical and cultural landscape. New lifestyles will emerge; the people will have new aspirations and different expectations. Value systems may undergo transformation. For better or for worse, norms may change and shifting mores will give a new dimension to our collective consciousness of shared values. Increasing affluence will give rise to greater litigation consciousness, greater awareness of individual rights and the civil remedies available; and certainly an increase in activity in all fields of endeavour, more inter-country links and travel across national borders. These in turn will give rise to increased legal complications and, *ipso facto*, the role of lawyers will become more significant.

As the region continues to progress, the necessity to understand each other's legal and judicial systems becomes all the more pressing. For instance, the harmonization of laws in the Asean region is a pressing issue. Being largely linked to the socio-political aims of Asean as a supra-national entity, it has of course to be resolved through the political forum. From the legal viewpoint, the process of harmonizing will certainly strike certain discordant notes, considering the variety of legal systems involved. Lessons could easily be drawn from the European Union where fundamental issues of legal sovereignty have, until today, not been resolved.

In the context of Malaysia, our experience has shown that failure to keep abreast with the developments in the law in other jurisdictions has resulted in retrogressive judgments from our own courts. This state of affairs has been blamed on certain provisions of the Civil Law Act, which have led to the ossification of judicial thinking. This form of legislative enslavement is one legacy of the colonial past from which we must liberate ourselves. For example, certain features of the English Common Law, the foundation of the Malaysian legal system, are archaic and irrelevant to our society. The fact that they continue to be part of the legal corpus manifests jurisprudential malaise on the part of our law-makers. Thus, progressive reforms should be instituted to enable the legal system of each country to develop in tandem with the overall progress of the society.

Muslim countries, too, continue to suffer from this colonial legacy. In Malaysia's case, the Shariah (Divine Law) system dealing almost exclusively with Islamic Family Law, and meant only for the adjudication and administration of justice among Muslims, exists side by side with the civil law system inherited from British colonial rule. Much of the laws of pre-colonial times based on Islamic jurisprudence and the customs of the people were replaced by colonial legislation based on the English Common Law. This has given rise to conflicts of laws on account of the clash of jurisdictions between two separate and distinct legal systems, each deriving their principles and values from different sources. Such instances may be rare, but when they do occur, they invariably result in injustice. As justice is the ultimate end of the judicial process, much needs to be done in order to harmonize the laws and eliminate the potentialities of such conflicts.

The dynamic growth of our laws should entail the ability to draw upon the wealth of laws in other jurisdictions as well as from other legal systems. To ensure legislative dynamism, certain key areas of the law need to be thoroughly reviewed, either by way of repealing old laws or introducing new ones. In such a time as we are in, where industrialization and economic development is moving at a rapid pace, laws pertaining to commercial transactions and cross-border arrangements, multimedia and cyberlaws, penal law and the sentencing system, need to be revised regularly.

While economic prosperity is an essential ingredient of a successful society, neither nation-building nor the happiness of our society can be realized through the fulfillment of material needs alone. The moral and cultural dimensions are equally essential. The notion of accountability, which is one of the hallmarks of a morally responsible government, requires us to heed the voices of those who have been unjustly or unfairly treated. All the great traditions of mankind enjoin the dispensation of justice to all. For instance, in the Islamic tradition, causing injustice to another person is clearly prohibited. As the Prophet of Islam commanded: "*lā yazlimuhu wa lā yakhdhuluhu* – neither be unjust to him nor abandon him."[9] To reach a golden age of justice, it is crucial that this sense of justice be imbued among all those involved in the legal and judicial system. Law teachers, parliamentary draughtsmen, legal advisors to government departments, prosecutors, advocates and solicitors, magistrates, registrars and above all, judges, must have a strong sense of justice.

Concepts of justice must have hands and feet or they remain sterile abstractions. This means that there must be efficient means and methods to carry out justice in every case in the shortest possible time and at the lowest possible cost. There must also be introspective reviews of existing laws and legislations to see that we have not backslided or compromised our ideals of justice, and that we keep in step with the progress of civilization. If the law does not keep abreast with the march of time, it will soon be rendered archaic and obsolete. To quote the words of the late Supreme Court Justice Eusoffe Abdoolcader:

> Even if the law's pace may be slower than society's march, what with increased and increasing civic-consciousness and appreciation of rights and fundamental values in the citizenry, it must nonetheless strive to be relevant if it is to perform its function of peaceful ordering of the relations between and among persons in society, and between and among persons and government at various levels.[10]

---

Endnotes

1 Freeman, M.D.A., *Lloyd's Introduction to Jurisprudence*, sixth edition, London: Sweet and Maxwell Ltd, 1994, p. 136.

2 *Ibid.*, p. 87.

3 Tocqueville, Alexis de, *Democracy in America*, New York: Alfred A. Knopf, 1963.

4 *al Nisa* 4:58.

5 Freeman, M.D.A., *op. cit.*, p. 87.

6   Rawls, John, *A Theory of Justice*, Cambridge: Harvard University Press, 1971. See also *Political Liberalism*, New York: Columbia University Press, 1996, by the same author.

7   Posner, Richard, *The Essential Holmes*, Chicago: Chicago University Press, 1992, p. 161.

8   Howard, Philip K., *The Death of Common Sense*, New York: Random House, 1994, p. 44.

9   Hadith narrated by Muslim.

10  Tan Sri Hj Othman Saat v Mohd bin Ismail (1982) 2 Malayan Law Journal, p. 179.

# Ethics and Economics

Some time in the early years of the eighteenth century, there appeared on the streets of London a sixpenny pamphlet, published anonymously, that was destined to cause the scandal of the century. Titled *The Grumbling Hive; or Knaves Turned Honest*, it was later described as the "wickedest cleverest book in the English Language." Bernard Mandeville, who subsequently surfaced as the author of the pamphlet, admitted that the work was mere doggerel. Yet it was a most damning assault on social ethics. Thus he mocked:

> The root of Evil, Avarice,
> That damn'd ill-natur'd baneful Vice,
> Was Slave to Prodigality,
> That noble Sin; Whilst Luxury
> Employed a Million of the Poor,
> And Odious Pride a Million more:
> Envy itself, and Vanity,
> Were ministers of Industry;
> Their darling Folly, Fickleness,

In Diet, Furniture and Dress,
That strange ridic'lous Vice, was made
The very Wheel that turn'd the Trade.[1]

The playfulness of these "loose lines", as Mandeville called them, was a masquerade for the proposition that was later brought to bear on various disciplines of learning, including philosophy and ethics. But its lasting impact was on the emerging field of study called economics; greed, vanity and envy were to be celebrated as the quintessence of beneficence to society at large. Self-interest, not altruism, was the key to the promotion of wealth and prosperity, and any form of government control and regulation was suspect.

Ultimately, it required periodic hard knocks to restore balance and to drive home the point that a society without any means of checking private greed would suffer dire consequences. One should not underestimate the power of greed, for when it comes to it, even geniuses can be fools. Sir Isaac Newton capitulated to greed and folly in the South Seas speculative hysteria and lost £20,000. Later, in a more sober mood, he was reported to have said: "I can measure the motions of the bodies, but I cannot measure human folly."[2]

We succumb to folly the moment we throw prudence and common sense to the wind. Zeal may be a virtue, but over-zealousness is a vice that springs from a simplistic mindset, which gives rise to the periodic pendulum swings in economic policy. Whether it is blind faith in market-driven solutions or reverent belief in government as the sole arbiter on the production and distribution of goods, both attitudes suffer from the naïveté that there are simple prescriptions to complex societal problems. It takes a strong sense of realism underlined by humility to avoid such pendulum swings and to keep us on the middle path – the Islamic *awsaṭuhā*, the *chun yung* of Confucius or the golden mean of Aristotle. And consistent with our vision of integral man, only by taking the middle path can one address economic problems as human problems and do justice to its manifold dimensions.

## FAILURE OF MARXISM

Marxism burst onto the world stage with the victory of the Bolsheviks in Russia in 1917, inspired by an economic theory and a programme which promised nothing less than paradise on earth – the eradication of all social classes, economic equality and freedom from all forms of tyranny. The state was henceforth to be governed by "the dictatorship of the proletariat", the ordinary working people who had always been subject to various forms of exploitation by the ruling classes. Now for the first time, they were to have a real say in the affairs of society. However, Marxism failed precisely because of its flawed vision of man. It severs man from his moorings in faith, viewing him as nothing more than a cypher, a cog in a brutal machine called the state. There was no place for ethics, morality or spirituality. Lenin said there was in Marxism "not a grain of ethics from beginning to end." Morality was served to "destroy the old exploiting society ... We do not believe in an eternal morality and we expose the falseness of all the fables about morality."[3]

The economic reasons for the collapse of the Marxist state are obvious. It is in essence a command economy, structured like a military organization, rather than a system involving the voluntary and spontaneous interaction of countless individuals as economic agents. Production and distribution – what to produce and who gets what – are determined by bureaucrats, not to meet the needs of the citizenry but the needs of the state as they are perceived by the *nomenklatura*. The crucial role of the price system as transmitter and processor of information was suppressed, resulting in severe distortions. Consumer choice was limited in the sense that individuals were free only to choose between goods supplied by the planners to the state stores, and production was not organized to respond to shortages or surpluses.

The appeal of Marxism to developing countries was due largely to its anti-imperialist rhetoric. For countries that had been tyrannized and exploited by colonialism, Marxism provided the impetus to galvanize the masses into action. Marxist ideas supplied the analytical tools to grasp and articulate the predicament of post-colonial societies. It offered guidance in every department of a man's activities, with specific, ready-made solutions for almost every political problem. The certitude and comprehensiveness of Marxism were comforting to people disoriented by the often bloody passage from colony to independent nation. Intoxicated with Marxist ideas, Third World leaders concocted national ideologies to justify and rationalize revolutionary social experiments. In Asia and Africa, Marxism and socialism mutated into a number of variants. In West Asia, Arab Socialism (*al-ishtirākiyya al-ᶜarabiyya*) was propagated as a programme of social and political reform. In Indonesia, Sukarno launched what he called Marhaenism (from Marhaen, a common name in Java), a type of Marxist socialism adapted to the Indonesian community and spirit. He also conceived NASAKOM, a fusion of nationalism, religion and communism, the major revolutionary streams that earlier overthrew the Dutch. In Tanzania, Julius Nyerere constructed a national programme called *ujamaa* or 'familyhood', a combination of socialism and African social and political structure. In practice, however, it was as anti-family as any other totalitarian ideology; *ujamaa* was merely a euphemism for forced collectivization, an elaborate and sanctimonious authoritarian philosophy.

The general conclusion that can be drawn from the experience of the developing countries is that there is an inverse relationship between national success and socialism. Socialism directly contributed to the pauperization of the masses.

Marxism was also linked to the rise of liberation theology and the *dependencia* school of development economics which perceived conventional economic growth as increasing the dependency of developing countries on the capitalistic metropolises located in the North. Leftists also seized on a report published by the Club of Rome (not an organization known to be sympathetic to Marxist economic theories and prescriptions) called *The Limits to Growth*, which was the watermark of the anti-growth movement.[4] The report contributed immensely to the consciousness of the harmful effects of the growth mania on the environment. It purported to demonstrate scientifically the disastrous consequences of high growth rates to the global economy: the world would quickly exhaust its vital resources of raw material and food supplies, while the environment would be irreversibly degraded. The report caught the attention of the public, and was initially accepted as constituting a scientific demonstration of the need for governments to slow down growth rates. But the serious defect of its methodology soon became apparent and its conclusions were challenged in key aspects. Besides, the report presented only the perspective of the industrialized world. True, while the industrialized countries were burdened by excessive growth, the developing world suffered from insufficient growth and stagnating economies. As such, the report had little to offer poor countries whose citizens could not possibly have sleepless nights worrying about what would happen to the world by the year 2050, when they were not even sure they would get a decent meal the next day.

In recalling the rise and fall of Communism, we hope to derive some important lessons. First, ideals and good intentions by themselves are not enough to achieve noble ends. We must also be very clear about the means of attaining our declared objectives. We must not barter the good which is real, though imperfect, with something which appears perfect, but turns out to be illusory. Secondly, we can learn that no collectivity built upon violence can hope to avoid an equally violent reversal in the course of time.

## THE COUNTER-REVOLUTION

Since the 1980s, global public opinion has swung back in favour of the invisible hand. Today, the world has once again fallen in love with the market-place. In the industrial countries, the welfare system is under attack. Upon the insistence of the industrial world, multilateral agencies are prescribing, with religious zeal, macroeconomic stabilization as the cure-all for economic ills. Thus they enjoin: "Thou shalt privatize, thou shalt deregulate, and thou shalt not interfere in the market." However, while free trade and competition are highly valued by industrialized countries as rhetorical devices, they have not been the notable features of their practice except when expedient.

While the positive aspects of the return of the market in economic management are obvious, the capitalist counter-revolution is in danger of swinging to the other extreme. Affirmative action is denounced as misplaced compassion, undermining personal responsibility. Social agenda such as public housing, health care for the poor and the fairer distribution of economic opportunities, are relegated to the periphery. Sophisticated new arguments are being put forth to prove the virtue of the market and the harm of intervention, however well-intended. One of them is the concept of the rationality of the market: leave it alone, and the market will behave according to our rational expectations. But this dogma simply cannot stand up to scrutiny. Regular bouts of financial frenzy leading to panic and crises are testimony that the markets are not insulated from irrational behaviour. Markets are but a body of human beings engaged in complex economic transactions and in a group, the herd instinct often predominates. "Anyone taken as an individual," noted Friedrich von Schiller, "is tolerably sensible and reasonable. As a member of a crowd, he at once becomes a blockhead."[5]

Unfettered growth is now hailed as the magic wand of economic policy. Let there be growth, for growth will create wealth, eliminate poverty, improve living conditions and expand choice. The power of growth to transform society from poverty to prosperity cannot be denied, and nowhere is this process more remarkable than in East Asia. In the 1970s and 1980s, average per capita income grew by seven per cent annually, the most sustained and widespread development of the century, perhaps in all of history. These countries have in 30 years achieved progress in human development that took industrial countries more than 100 years. Living standards for hundreds of millions have risen. Basic education and literacy have spread significantly. Mortality rates for infants, children and women have fallen. Access to safe water and sanitation has greatly increased. And the gender gap in basic human capabilities has narrowed considerably, even though significant gaps in opportunities remain.

Despite this stunning progress, however, many forms of deprivation remain. In East Asia, in 1990, nearly 170 million people were living below the poverty line, and more than 100 million boys and girls were out of school at the secondary level. In Southeast Asia and the Pacific, more than a third of children under five are malnourished and nearly one million children in East Asia die before the age of five. It may be argued that in due time and with more growth, these ills will be eliminated. That is likely to be wishful thinking, otherwise industrial countries would be free of such problems. Yet, today, more than 100 million people in the industrial countries live below the poverty line, and more than five million are homeless.

## THE MIDDLE PATH

Economic policy must relate itself to the social realities of each society and its peculiar needs. If any lesson is to be drawn from the economic performance of East Asia during the last three decades, it is that the invisible and the visible hands must work together. The imperative is to strike a balance between market forces and benign intervention.

Perhaps no other religion has put more confidence in the market than Islam. When prices rose and the Prophet was asked to intervene, he replied: "God is the controller of prices."[6] As historian Ibn Khaldun noted, Islamic civilization was marked by a pervasive commercial spirit where the market thrived. The Muslim mind is nurtured to be pro-market. Quranic injunctions are often couched in commercial imagery. A successful merchant in his younger years, the Prophet's understanding of the workings of the market came from first-hand experience. The formative period of Islamic law, too, coincided with a period of lively commercial activity and some prominent jurists were themselves traders, thus imbuing the laws with flexibility and a sense of realism.

Despite this favourable disposition towards the market, Muslim societies in the past saw the need to introduce the institution called *hisba* to oversee fairness in market dealings, to check against monopoly and manipulation. The rebuke of the Quran against the accumulation of wealth among a privileged class, "that wealth would not circulate among a few" provides a sense of balance in the Muslim mind and lays the foundation for the principle of distributive justice. These teachings help to nurture the growth of social institutions for mutual help in hard times and for the protection of the poor, the needy, orphans and widows. Foremost among them is the institution of *zakāt*, a tithe on income, property, agriculture and business, to be distributed to assist those in need. Another unique institution of Muslim society is the *waqf*, a charitable foundation which finances the growth of hospitals, universities and scholarly pursuits.

Thus, the issue today is not whether to grow or not to grow. Growth is necessary. The debate should instead be focused on the kind of growth that we want. The Human Development Report 1996 has classified six types of growth with negative consequences which must be avoided. First, *jobless growth*, where the overall economy grows but does not expand the opportunities for employment, as experienced by several OECD countries in 1993. Second, *ruthless growth*, where the fruits of economic growth mostly benefit the rich, leaving millions mired in ever deepening poverty. Third, *voiceless growth*, which does not empower the people and which silences alternative voices. Fourth, *rootless growth*, which causes the people's cultural identity to wither. And finally, *futureless growth*, where the present generation squanders the resources needed by future generations.[7]

Economic growth has to be integrated in the overall philosophy of human development. The final aim of economic pursuit is the development of man, not the Promethean man of secular humanism who relentlessly seeks to conquer, but rather man as envisaged by the great traditions of East and West. In the language of Confucianism, it is the Perfect Man or *chun tzu*, the morally perfect being who always stands in awe of Heaven or the Superior Man, *jen*, who is loyal to his moral nature (*chung*) and treats others as himself (*shu*). Such a man finds his parallel in the Islamic tradition as *insān sālih*, the Virtuous Man.

The renewal of interest in the relevance of the ethical dimension in the discourse on economics, departing from the conventional enquiry founded upon the idea of *homo economicus* in pursuit of self-interest, is in part inspired by a rediscovery of the moral philosophy of Adam Smith in its more integral form. While the founder of the discipline of economics has been largely credited with the discovery of self-interest as the engine of wealth accumulation, he himself considered "wisdom and virtue" more worthy of admiration than material riches.

> This disposition to admire, and almost to worship, the rich and the powerful, and to despise, or, at least to neglect persons of poor and mean condition, though necessary both to establish and maintain the distinction of rank and order of society, is, at the same time, the great and most universal cause of the corruption of our moral sentiments. The wealth and greatness are often regarded with the respect and admiration which are due only to wisdom and virtue; and the contempt, of which vice and folly are the only proper objects, is often most unjustly bestowed upon poverty and weakness, has been the complaint of moralists in all ages.[8]

By asserting the primacy of moral values and taking cognizance that man and society are engaged in a perpetual struggle of conscience, Adam Smith was expounding an ethical philosophy which echoed that of the great minds of the past, including Ibn Khaldun, the Muslim philosopher, and Wang An Shih, the Confucian reformer. The challenge for us is to rededicate ourselves to this holistic approach towards growth and development.

## Endnotes

1   Mandeville, Bernard, *Fable of the Bees, Vol. I*, edited by F.B. Kaye, Indianapolis: Liberty Classic, 1988.

2   Galbraith, John Kenneth, *A Short History of Financial Euphoria*, New York: Viking, 1993.

3   Lenin, *Collected Works*, cited in Lloyd's *Introduction to Jurisprudence*, sixth edition, by M.D.A. Freeman, London: Sweet and Maxwell Ltd, 1994.

4   Meadows, Donella H., Meadows, Dennis L., Randers, Jorgen, W. Behreeus III, William, *The Limits to Growth, A Report for the Club of Rome's Project on the Predicament of Mankind*, London: Pan Books, 1972.

5   Quoted by Hayek, F.A., *The Road to Serfdom*, Chicago: University of Chicago Press, 1972.

6   Hadith narrated by Ibnu Majah.

7   *UNDP Human Development Report 1996*, New York: Oxford University Press, 1996.

8   Smith, Adam, *The Theory of Moral Sentiments*, edited by D.D. Raphael and A.L. Macfie, Oxford: Clarendon Press, 1976, pp. 61–62.

# The Humane Economy

Underpinning a humane economy is a philosophy of development which is holistic, guided by ethical and social concerns and founded upon the principles of justice and virtue (*al-ᶜadl wa 'l-iḥsān*). Managing such an economy is not only about the allocation of scarce resources to satisfy man's physical and material needs. It is also about the allocation of those same resources to satisfy man's spiritual and intellectual wants.

This does not mean that the spirit of enterprise ought to be dampened or that the pursuit of material wealth and comfort is to be frowned upon. Indeed, they should be encouraged, for the needs of earthly subsistence must be satisfied before the attainment of the higher goals of the spirit and the intellect is possible.

## PRODUCTIVITY

Although deficit spending to boost economic performance has been made respectable by Keynesian orthodoxy, the key to sustainable economic growth is still productivity. The post-Second World War economic histories of Japan and Britain are instructive. Victorious Britain failed to prepare its workforce with the skills and technology required in the highly competitive global arena of the 1980s and 1990s, especially without the ability to continue tapping, at minimal costs, the resources of its erstwhile colonies.

Defeated Japan, on the other hand, invested heavily in skills-building, research and other programmes to maximize productivity and make up for its lack of natural resources. As a result, Japan's productivity growth has averaged about 7 per cent a year since the end of the war while Britain's average is only about 1.5 per cent. Thus, Britain, one of the leading world economies in the first half of this century, is now trailing far behind Japan as an economic power.

The singular importance of productivity in improving human welfare is demonstrated by the emergence of the Newly Industrializing Countries (NICs) in East Asia. In these countries, education and training have been, and continue to be, a major priority in resource allocation.

In many developing countries, the basic infrastructure needs to be modernized and the rural sector must be integrated into the mainstream of economic development. The economy must continue to expand, for stagnation – or even slow growth – would only perpetuate misery and delay social progress. The move towards free markets is therefore to be lauded, but one must caution against the unleashing of the forces of supply and demand onto an economy that is ill-prepared. Free markets must come about gradually, steered steadily towards an environment conducive to the promotion of social justice. Public funds would need to be expended towards the growth of human capital, chiefly through education and health care, and towards poverty eradication and the creation of humane living and working conditions.

One of the greatest deceptions in our time is that reckless spending, sheer waste and extravagance is justified in the name of social responsibility. Under the pretext of welfare programmes to help the poor and the disadvantaged, huge bureaucracies are set up whose operating costs eat up as much as 75 per cent of the money allocated.

Even if one rules out profligacy and blatant financial mismanagement, there is still the risk of failure due to unexpected events. Such failures can be avoided if strategic planning is applied, factoring all possible contingencies. Of even greater importance is economic planning with a clear social programme, without which a civil society cannot emerge. Developing economies in Asia have dealt with the issue pragmatically by committing the government's resources to an effective social agenda encompassing poverty eradication, public health and housing, and substantive investment in human resource development. The more successful economies of the region had early on determined that their priorities lay in the provision of free primary education for all, affordable health and medical facilities, and basic public utilities and communications and transport infrastructure. The overriding objective of such programmes should be the reduction of disparities between the rich and the poor and the provision of social mobility through training and employment opportunities.

The attainment of such long-term objectives warrants commitment to certain sound principles and rules. This entails limiting the discretionary spending powers of the government of the day. Governments with unfettered discretion in this regard are likely to be dictated by short-term pressures and political expediency, rather than be guided by rules which embody the experience accumulated over a long period.

## TAXATION

In the realm of fiscal policy, governments have long been confounded by the problem of how to raise the maximum amount of revenue with the minimum of hardship to the people.

Experience has shown that progressive reduction of taxes does not necessarily lead to a reduction in revenues. On the contrary, with an efficient tax collection system, tax reduction can lead to an increase in the amount of revenue collected. This principle was observed some 500 years ago by a great Muslim thinker and a precursor of many modern economic ideas, ᶜAbd al-Rahman ibn Khaldun. In his magnum opus, the *Muqaddimah* or *Introduction to History*, Ibn Khaldun wrote:

> When tax assessments and imposts upon the subjects are low, the latter have the energy and desire to do things. Cultural enterprises grow and increase, because the low taxes bring satisfaction. When cultural enterprises grow, the number of individual imposts and assessments mounts. In consequence, the tax revenue, which is the sum total of (the individual assessments), increases ... (However, when) the assessments increase beyond the limits of equity, the result is that the interest of the subjects in cultural enterprises disappears, since when they compare expenditures and taxes with their income and gain and see the little profit they make, they lose all hope. Therefore, many of them refrain from all cultural activity. The result is that the total tax revenue goes down, as individual assessments go down.[1]

This doctrine, however appealing, cannot be taken at face value, for underlying it is the principle of fiscal discipline. By not cutting spending in tandem with tax reductions, the United States went, in just one decade, from being the world's largest creditor nation to being the largest debtor. The lesson from the American experience is that once budget deficits become chronic, the economy will be trapped in a vicious circle. Government budget deficits directly affect both the level of aggregate demand and its composition. Hence, they tend to be inflationary. In general, larger deficits lead to higher interest rates at any level of GNP, reduce the share of GNP devoted to investment, and increase the share devoted to consumption and government spending. To the extent that investment is crowded out by higher interest rates, the future capital stock will be smaller, thus reducing future real income and consumption. Large budget deficits impair economic growth by reducing national saving and capital formation. Deficits also create a vicious circle of more government borrowing and higher debt service costs, which in turn make it still more difficult to reduce the deficit.

Deficits to finance investment on infrastructure development and research activities can be justified on the ground that they contribute to increasing future productivity. But most of the time, a deficit is not caused by expenditure on such activities but rather on expenditure that has no contribution to increasing productivity. Military spending is a case in point. For most countries, industrial or developing, military spending has been the single most important contributor to deficits. Fiscal problems are particularly more pronounced in countries caught up in the arms race. The extreme case was the Soviet Union, where the militarization of the economy sapped the nation of its resources and became the fundamental cause for its collapse. Another example of prodigality would be spending binges on prestige projects which do not add value to the economy but, like cosmetic surgery, merely beautify the facade to satisfy the vanity of human wishes.

The only way to break out of this circle is by balancing the budget. This means cutting spending to match revenues. Managing the finances of a country is like managing the household. As stated by Adam Smith, "What is prudence in the conduct of every private family, can scarce be folly in that of a great kingdom."[2] Even with sustained economic growth, there is always the need to be mindful of the eternal lesson, taught in the Quranic story of the Prophet Yusuf (Joseph in the Bible), that the years of plenty may be followed by lean and trying times. It is, therefore, our own negligence, profligacy and poor planning that are usually to blame for economic disaster, not the accidents of nature or the vagaries of life.

## PRIVATIZATION

The primary rationale for privatization is to transfer, from the public sector to the private sector, the burden of incurring huge capital outlays and operating costs normally required of large scale national projects and undertakings. Freed of this burden, the public sector would be strategically positioned to allocate scarce financial and human resources to implement the higher ideals of economic management, that is, the realization of social agenda programmes.

Privatization is also the obvious answer to bloated public sector agencies. This solution is particularly needed in the case of developing countries where it is not uncommon to find such agencies, more often than not, transmuted into unwieldy colossuses, unable to keep pace with the demands of changing realities. Such bureaucracies, characterized by top heavy management, overstaffing and absence of dynamic entrepreneurial leadership, are not only inefficient but perform dismally in terms of the bottom line. Experience has shown that such agencies are not averse to incurring huge losses, getting scandal-ridden and becoming a major source of embarrassment to the government of the day.

Notwithstanding the virtues of privatization, a caveat must be lodged at the outset. Privatized entities must be fully conscious of their social responsibility. Measures must be instituted and moral suasion exercised to ensure that privatized entities and beneficiaries of the policy are not driven solely by profit motives. Privatization has to be transparent and subject to a regulatory framework, lest the public fall prey to corporate Titans ganging up to form monopolies. According to Adam Smith, "People of the same trade seldom meet together, even for merriment and diversion, but the conversation ends in a conspiracy against the public, or in some contrivance to raise prices."[3] The government should be pro-business, but businesses must have a human face. Conglomerates cannot be allowed to grow into banyan trees under which no others can flourish. The private sector is encouraged to undertake projects such as poverty eradication, education, health and public housing. Unregulated privatization is fertile ground for monopoly and other forms of rent seeking behaviour to thrive.

## CORRUPTION AND MISMANAGEMENT

Corruption, which includes abuse of monopolistic power, cronyism and nepotism, exacts social costs on society. Any proposition that corruption should be tolerated as a necessary evil in promoting growth ought to be rejected. Corruption, legalized or not, is a moral issue. The great Chinese reformer, Wang An Shih (1021–1086), in his attempt to stamp out corruption, was impressed by two ever-recurrent sources of corruption, bad laws and bad men. Ibn Khaldun, during his appointment as a judge, tried to eliminate corruption and considered that the root cause of corruption was the passion for luxurious living within the ruling group.[4]

True, the problem of corruption has been with mankind from time immemorial and is not something that can be eliminated overnight. But that is no excuse for not making a serious commitment to fight it. The issue may be a moral one, but effective measures against corruption must go beyond mere moralizing to encompass comprehensive societal and legal reform. There must be the political will to wage war against this insidious blight of mankind, a war backed by the full force of the law. The main actors in the circle of the corrupt must be prosecuted in a judicial system marked by integrity and moral courage in its deliberations.

In a humane economy, therefore, there is optimum utilization of scarce resources, discipline in fiscal management, promotion of a clear social agenda, and a profound respect for the environment. The prudent use of resources entails the protection and conservation of the environment for the benefit of future generations. Natural disasters arising from the pillage and plunder of the earth must not be attributed to "acts of God" when in fact they are but the revenge of nature on man's avarice and arrogance.

Endnotes

1   Ibn Khaldun, *Muqaddimah*, translated by Franz Rosenthal, London: Routledge and Kegan Paul in association with Secker and Warburg, 1987, Chapter Three, pp. 230–231.

2   Smith, Adam, *The Wealth of Nations* in *Great Books of the Western World Vol. 36,* edited by Mortimer J. Adler, Chicago: Encyclopaedia Britannica, Inc.,1991, Book Four, Chapter II, p. 218.

3   *Ibid*, Book One, Chapter X, p. 63.

4   Alatas, Syed Hussein, *The Problem of Corruption,* Singapore: Times Books International, 1989.

# The Primacy of Culture

In the late part of 1994 an international conference on literature was held in Kuala Lumpur on the theme "Ethnocentric Perspectives in Literature". A chorus of attack was heard against the "Canon" and particular texts by Western writers were singled out as classic examples of cultural imperialism in literature. Typical of such debates, charges of male chauvinism, racism, anti-minoritism and cultural separatism flew like sparks, and at the end of the proceedings there was a call for a reevaluation of the established texts and a redefinition of the Canon.

There is nothing new about the passion and often, the hysteria that literature tends to generate. Matthew Arnold's *Culture and Anarchy* was essentially prompted by the fear that England was soon to be drowned by the rising tide of philistinism brought about by the growing affluent middle class who bore "a natural inaccessibility to ideas". T.S. Eliot, aided and abetted by F.R. Leavis, thought nothing of trying to dislodge Milton from the Canon altogether. Eliot himself is now the subject of renewed charges of anti-Semitism.

If literature is to be viewed as the voice of a community, it is not difficult to understand the clamour for close readings and ethnocentric viewpoints. At least in the Asian context, this was an upshot of the decolonization process, wherein the burning desire to assert one's identity reigned supreme. These were the voices of protest – against domination, exploitation and other forms of oppression. For those who have had to endure the whips and scorns of marginalization and victimization, the idea of cultivating one's own view does seem rather invigorating. It certainly holds out the prospects of literary empowerment. That means the power to choose who, what and how to read. It means there is more to the Canon than a list of books by dead white males – Dante and Dostoevsky, Kafka and Kierkegaard, Shakespeare and Stendhal, Tolstoy and Twain, and so on. But with power, there is always a possibility of abuse, and one should be reminded of the exhortation by Edward Said of the pitfalls of compromising one's intellectual integrity for the cause of "defensive, reactive and even paranoid nationalism".[1] This is notwithstanding that he himself is an arch critic of the cultural imperialism of Western art and literature. Overzealous nationalism is also a theme imaginatively explored by Ali Mazrui in *The Trial of Christopher Okigbo*, in which after his death, the protagonist has to answer why, in his earthly life as a poet, he had subjected his art to the narrowness of tribalism.

Of course, one has to fight to be heard. But to abandon the need for discernment between the good and the bad, between the superior and the mediocre, solely because we demand to be heard, is a new form of enslavement. As Matthew Arnold says: "But the aspirations of culture, which is the study of perfection, are not satisfied, unless what men say, when they may say what they like, is worth saying."[2] If the discourse on literature is merely about taste, then every man hence to his idle bed – *de gustibus non est disputandum*. We have to separate the wheat from the chaff as indeed, there is literature and there are books, and the two shall never meet. For reasons of cultural and ethnic diversity, literary standards may, and indeed do, differ. But whether the emphasis should be on cognitive acuity, linguistic energy or power of imagination, all great literary works must withstand the test of time. Even as we pamper ourselves with the appreciation of the great works, we ought not shut our minds to the emergence of the new literatures. Great literature emancipates and does not enslave. It is noteworthy that Harold Bloom's *The Western Canon* includes literature of the ancient near East, ancient India, and classical Arabic as part of the Canon. While we are quite familiar with, and may even have grown accustomed to, the anti-Islamic rhetoric of the West, the following remarks of Bloom's bear repetition:

> ... once the reader is conversant with the Bible, Homer, Plato, the Athenian dramatists and Virgil, the crucial work is the Koran. Whether for its aesthetic and spiritual power or the influence it will have upon all our futures, ignorance of the Koran is foolish and increasingly dangerous.[3]

No doubt, the debate will continue, and it is not without its intrinsic value. For one, it helps to deconstruct certain myths. For instance, Western literature has characteristically painted Islam as a religion of destruction. Art and culture critic Robert Hughes debunks this in the following terms:

> Historically, Islam the Destroyer is a myth. Without Arab scholars, our mathematics would not exist and only a fraction of the Greek intellectual heritage would have come down to us. Medieval Rome was a scavengers' village compared with medieval Baghdad. Without the Arab invasion of southern Spain or el-Andalus ... the culture of southern Europe would be unimaginably poorer.[4]

But the more pressing concern of our society today is to arrest the waning interest in literature itself. In general, there appears to be a preoccupation with pursuing the mundane and the merely utilitarian. Shops selling stationery are masquerading as bookshops. In so called conventional bookstores, management pundits and spiritual-success gurus sell like hot cakes. Shakespeare does not. Neither does *Hikayat Hang Tuah* nor *Sejarah Melayu*. Even as we are becoming richer economically, we are becoming poorer culturally. Like England in the nineteenth century, our society is now being threatened by a rising tide of philistinism. Culture "has always a rough task to achieve" anywhere, but particularly in East Asia, where people are caught up in the quest for wealth and worldly comfort as never before. Apart from religion, it is literature that will enable us to regain the fullness of our humanity. Literature, according to Lionel Trilling, is the human activity that takes the fullest and most precise account of variousness, possibility, complexity and difficulty.

The region is endowed with the necessary ingredients for the creation of a unique body of literature, simply by drawing upon the rich heritage of its cultural, religious and ethnic diversity. Given the right attitude and the requisite commitment, the possibilities for cultural enrichment through literature are indeed limitless. In the realm of education, measures should be taken to enable students to be exposed to the great works of world literature as early as possible. While ensuring that they are also well-entrenched in the traditional works, children must not continue to be force-fed a diet of trivia. If our creative potential is to be realized at all, we must emancipate ourselves from the narrow confines of ideology, gender, language or ethnicity. There must be a resolve to rise above mediocrity, break the habit of self-congratulation, and put an end to intellectual inbreeding.

## CULTURE VERSUS ECONOMICS

It may seem somewhat odd that in the age of economics, the primacy of culture is being stressed. Apart from the value of literature and the arts in the refinement of the human personality, the influence of cultural forces in shaping a new world order will become more prominent in the years to come. As William Blake says, "Empire follows Art, and not vice versa ..." Likewise, the re-ordering of the global environment must be preceded by the changing balance of cultural influence. Not only has Asia to fortify itself against the possibility of negative cultural bombardment, it has to be able to make a positive and lasting contribution to a new world civilization which is just and equitable.

Trade and commerce is no longer a simple matter of supply and demand of goods and services. Values invariably come into play. True, the protectionist linking of trade with non-economic issues is not justified, but commerce and culture cannot be wholly separated. Even if the driving force of our time and in the foreseeable future shall be predominantly economics, it alone cannot solve all problems. Strong moral fibre, a sense of solidarity, and the life of the arts and imagination are no less crucial than material wealth in ensuring the sustainability of society. If we conceive our future to be holistic and multidimensional, the moral and cultural consequences of that vocation are inevitable.

In its earlier encounter with the powerful West, Asia often found refuge in its diverse and rich spiritual and cultural heritage. Now that it has gained a new sense of confidence in its economic potential and capability, it must guard against a Faustian bargain. A holistic concept of economic development, infused with humanitarian values, should be advocated. Even as pragmatic and utilitarian policies are set in addressing current challenges, the ultimate goal is moral and ethical progress. As economic and commercial linkages with other nations are being forged, Asia should coterminously seek to enhance cultural intercourse. It is inevitable that questions such as human rights and the environment, for example, will be examined in such encounters, but this should be done with genuine empathy.

More than two decades ago, the great Japanese novelist, Yasunari Kawabata, proclaimed the twenty-first century to be the Asian century. His vision was indeed bold, for most Asian countries were then in their early stages of national reconstruction, and a few were yet to experience their worst conflicts and calamities. From the vantage point of our time, his vision was even more refreshing and profound because it went beyond economics, towards an Asia that would emerge as a major contributor to global civilization.

The idea of what constitutes Asia is elusive to some because of the diverse nature of Asian cultures. Yet, it is this very diversity that constitutes strength in a world increasingly threatened with the disappearance of cultural boundaries. The reflowering of Asian culture will be a powerful countermovement to the tendency towards homogenization, the cultural reductionism that comes with globalization. There is no point in being hysterical about international cable networks or being overawed by the threat of cultural domination via the web of the new electronic superhighways. The threat is real enough, but censorship and closing the sky is not the answer in this late twentieth century. Only creativity and imagination would provide Asian societies with cultural empowerment, not only to withstand the new and more subtle forms of domination, but equally to offer the world their own cultural output.

The great irony about Asia is that its great thinkers and works of art and literature had to be "discovered" by the West first before they could reach a wider audience among Asians themselves.

Rabindranath Tagore and Kawabata would have remained largely obscure outside their countries, had it not been for the Nobel prize and the translations of their works into European languages. Therefore, there is an urgent need to promote Asian literature, arts and culture so as to foster a deeper understanding of ourselves and our own heritage. Only by doing so can Asians root out the reigning superficiality that breeds so much stereotyping about the West, producing unfruitful diatribes and rancorous disputes. The rhetoric against Western cultural products sometimes reaches the level of hysteria in our societies, often the result of our own folly, ineptness and want of discrimination. By pandering to philistine tastes and by becoming purveyors of the most banal and trivial output from the vast spectrum of Western cultures, Asians become easy, and perhaps justified, objects of loathing. They can have no one to blame but themselves if they continue to patronize trash, junk programmes and B-grade movies of the West at the expense of quality works of fellow Asians.

The challenge is to nurture an Asian *esthetique*. In recent times, one has witnessed the overwhelming diffusion of Western or Western-influenced cultural products. This has been made possible, and will be further accelerated, with the opening of the skies to satellite TV networks. It would not be too difficult for us to gain control of the communication technologies to empower ourselves with the means to mount a counter-offensive. Yet, that so-called empowerment would be meaningful only if we ourselves could offer cultural products that could compete for the attention of a discerning universal audience. Although the need for empowerment may not be as pressing and acute for certain Asian countries such as China, Japan and India, which have hitherto enjoyed the lion's share in Asia's quality cultural export to the West, it certainly is a crucial matter for the rest of Asia, particularly Southeast Asia.

## ASIAN VALUES AND CULTURAL ENGAGEMENT

What we envisage for Asia as a whole in the next century is that it should become a greater contributor to the advancement of human civilization. The Asian intellectual community must henceforth expend a significant part of its resources to nurturing and promoting the Asian heritage, especially those elements in the culture and traditions which not only characterize Asian identity but also contribute to the enrichment of a universal humane society. Among the elements, the most fundamental relate to the harmony of society through good governance, the sanctity of the family, tolerance towards diversity, and compassion for the weak and the unfortunate. While the objectives may coincide with those of others, Asia differs in emphases and approaches. Although it is open to learn from others, it is nevertheless justifiably convinced of the efficacy of its ways, because Asian cultures have survived largely intact for millenniums.

In the realm of civilizational encounters, Asia could take the lead in engaging the West in continuous dialogue, which is the *sine qua non* for the establishment of "the universal community of the human race". This requires, in the first place, a deeper appreciation, on the part of each of the great divides of humanity – East and West, North and South – of the values which the other side lives by. It is in literature that we will find the key to attain this goal. For only in the great literary works do we find reposed the noblest and most virtuous characters of humanity juxtaposed with the most depraved and the most vicious. It is of no consequence whether art imitates life, or life imitates art. Literature enables us to bridge the chasm of our individual separateness to partake in the universality of the human condition.

## CULTURE AND IDENTITY

The idea of a universal human community does not, however, mean the loss of separate identities. As a new consciousness of cultural identity among distinct groups in Asia, Africa, Latin America and the Caribbean gains ascendancy, efforts are being made to revitalize ancient traditions. More people are becoming disillusioned with "modernity", seeing it as nothing more than the contemporary development of but one particular culture, namely that of the West.

For the great majority of the world's population, the affirmation of a separate cultural identity through positive recognition of one's forebears may seem a simple matter of choice. In most cases, one simply *is* a Malay, Chinese, Indian, Thai, Filipino or whatever identity one assumes. However, for the indigenous people, chiefly of the entire American continent, and also of the rest of the non-Western world, the commemoration a few years back of the voyages of Christopher Columbus, voyages which initiated the age of Atlantic hegemony and the "universalization" of European culture, evoked a sense of great tragedy, and of the irreplaceable loss and desolation of entire ancient civilizations.

This tragedy is made vivid for us in the eye-witness account of Bartolomé de las Casas, who in 1502, participated in the Spanish conquest of Cuba, and saw the total massacre of an indigenous community. Writing 40 years later, he said:

> ... we know for sure that our fellow countrymen have, through their cruelty and wickedness, depopulated and laid waste an area which once boasted more than ten kingdoms, each of them larger in area than the Iberian peninsula.[5]

Las Casas estimated that over the 50 years after Columbus' historic journey, his compatriots had been responsible for the absolutely unwarranted deaths of almost 15 million indigenous people, including women and children.

What las Casas witnessed was perhaps the worst, but by no means, the last. Even today, in North America and some countries in the Pacific, the dominant populations have not quite reconciled themselves with their indigenous peoples. It is thus ironic that there should now be a global movement for indigenous people, whose focus is mainly directed towards the indigenous not in places where they suffer the worst atrocities, but in developing countries where they peacefully coexist with the larger population.

History is replete with instances of vested interests masquerading as altruism and humanitarian concern. It has been hardly 50 years since most developing countries liberated themselves from the yoke of colonialism carried out in the name of a civilizing mission. Even if some colonialists were genuinely altruistic, they could not liberate themselves from arrogance. John Stuart Mill, whose book *On Liberty* provided the intellectual foundation for the struggle for freedom, considered non-Western societies to be in a state of infancy, and thus had no right to liberty. According to Mill, "Despotism is a legitimate mode of government in dealing with Barbarians, provided the end be their improvement, and the means justified by actually effecting that end."[6]

In comparison with the brutalities inflicted by the colonial powers on indigenous populations elsewhere, British rule in Malaya was relatively humane. But that so-called humane policy also contributed to the perpetuation of socio-economic disparities along ethnic lines. In the name of protection, the Malays were confined to the rural areas for rice production. This policy was created and sustained by the colonial ideology based on the myth of "the lazy native".[7] At the same time, colonial policy on Malaya's

Orang Asli was formulated not for the sake of ensuring their progress, but solely in order to enlist their support against communist insurgents.

In Malaysia, the best course for the indigenous people is to accelerate integration into modern society. This warrants a readiness towards change on their part. Of course, this runs counter to the notion, promoted by a handful of international elites and organizations, that they would be better off in continued isolation from the rest of the world.

The advocates of a policy of isolation and benign neglect towards indigenous peoples must take a closer look at the state of indigenous communities within the advanced countries, particularly in North America and Australasia. Despite the geographical distance, they seem to suffer from a set of similar problems such as alcoholism, family breakdowns and general social malaise. This is characteristic of people who are demoralized and in a state of utter despair. They are looked upon by the rest of society with condescension, if not outright contempt. The blame lies squarely with the dominant society which has refused to acknowledge the equal humanity of the indigenous people and make them true partners in the political, economic and social process. A policy of isolation implies a refusal to contemplate a situation where the indigenous people may emerge as equal partners, neighbours and workmates.

Much of the current rhetoric on indigenous people almost exclusively focusing on issues of culture and identity, without paying serious attention to the real problems of development and the environment, is not only futile but harmful. It only encourages cultural separateness by exaggerating one's unique identity. This is understandable in situations where indigenous people have been subjected to oppression and humiliation, and treated as outcasts. But in Malaysia, for example, where plurality and multiculturality is the norm, the issue of a trade-off between identity and integration does not arise. One can be wholly integrated into the national mainstream, yet remain fully possessed of one's cultural specificity.

We need to be reminded of the danger of cutting oneself off from one's cultural roots by recounting a legendary tale among the Malays. It is the story of Si Tenggang, who is kidnapped, as a young boy, from his home in the rainforest by traders to be sold as a slave. However, by his wits and talents, he becomes not only a freeman but a man of wealth and power. In time, no one is left who knows of his origins. He himself has only a vague memory of his parents and childhood friends. He eventually marries the beautiful daughter of the king. One day, while on a pleasure cruise with his wife and her entourage, a fierce storm breaks out and forces him to take shelter close to his home in the forest. He is recognized and his overjoyed parents come out to greet him. But, ashamed of his roots, he disavows his links to them, and spurns his mother's profession of undying love and affection. The scorned mother, feeling betrayed and deeply hurt, then invokes the wrath of the gods on him. Retribution comes swiftly as Si Tenggang and his magnificent party are promptly turned to stone.

This legend underscores our abhorrence for those who would deny their identity for whatever reason. Thus, efforts to integrate indigenous people should not result in any loss of identity. Si Tenggang would not have been confronted by such a tragic situation if the so-called mainstream culture had treated the indigenous as equals in humanity and dignity.

## CULTURE AND THE LOVE FOR LEARNING

It has been said that you cannot see other cultures well until, through knowing your own, you reach a point where inclusiveness means something. Otherwise, you are left with mere indecisive mush. To do this, we must restore the central position of knowledge and learning in society. Teachers, scholars and intellectuals can all play their part to fire the passion of learning among the community and attract them to the *ladhdha al-ma‘rifa*, the pleasure of encountering great thoughts, the excitement of discovering new ideas. The Prophet of Islam said: "The superior rank the *‘alīm* holds in relation to the *‘abīd* is like the superior rank I hold in relation to the least of my companions."[8]

According to the celebrated littérateur and philologist, Abu Hilal al-Askari, the experience of the pleasure of knowledge is the highest form of pleasure, it is sublime and celestial. In his words:

> Since we have come to know the pleasure of knowledge,
> neither the sweet nor the tasty pleases us any more.[9]

Knowledge is the greatest of pleasures just as ignorance is the greatest of pains. Men of knowledge played a pivotal role in enabling Islam to produce one of the most dazzling civilizations ever known to humanity. At its height its wealth and power was unmatched, its beauty and splendour unrivalled. Despite all these, neither wealth nor power, neither the rich nor the powerful, enjoyed the prestige and stature equal to that of knowledge and men of learning be they *mufassirīn, muhaddithīn, fuqahā'*, philosophers, or poets who made Islamic civilization truly great. It was Ali ibn Abi Talib who said:

> *Yā kamīl!* Knowledge is better than wealth; for knowledge watches over you whilst you have to watch over your wealth. And knowledge governs while wealth is governed. Wealth diminishes with spending but knowledge increases therewith.[10]

As we enter the age of the information superhighway, we must guard against the confusion of information with knowledge. Explosion of information is not synonymous with explosion of knowledge. For information to be transformed into knowledge, one must have a unifying principle to distil and process it into an organized whole. Take away that principle and you will take away its soul. Where then is the knowledge we have lost in information?

Universities have to grow to be centres for the cultivation of the creative and adventurous mind. While pursuing specific interests, our minds must never be, to paraphrase Spanish intellectual José Ortega y Gasset, "barbarized" by specialization. We must remain alive to ideas from other disciplines and the general philosophic temper of the time.

Likewise, the American critic Allan Bloom chastises the contemporary American educational establishment for its preoccupation with the trivial and insignificant.

> ... the crisis of liberal education is a reflection of a crisis at the peaks of learning, an incoherence and incompatibility among the first principles with which we interpret the world, an intellectual crisis of the greatest magnitude, which constitutes the crisis of our civilization.[11]

Institutions of higher learning must have the desire and the capacity to venture boldly into the unexplored areas of philosophy and religion, law, economics, the arts and the sciences. Students must not be fed solely on a diet of textbooks, but guided to explore ideas from the works of the great masters, and to follow the disputes and controversies between rival schools and ultimately, enter yet greater treasure troves of knowledge. Yet, knowledge itself, without the requisite virtues such as humility, generosity, the love of truth and justice, will be, in the words of the poet-philosopher Muhammad Iqbal:

> as cold as death, like Satan's progeny ...
> But if it blends with love, it joins the ranks
> of high celestial spirits.[12]

The award of academic degrees to students who have been successful in their studies is a universal practice with its origins dating back from the third Hijriah century. The tradition and organization of colleges and universities, with academic freedom as one of their most treasured possessions, began in the medieval "licence to teach", known in Latin as the *licentia docendi*. Again, long before the *licentia docendi* appeared in the medieval Christian university, it had already developed in Islam, with the same designation, expressed in Arabic as *ijaza al-tadrīs*.

In our day, the authority to teach is conferred upon the doctoral candidate who has proven his scholastic competence in a field of study to which he has contributed an original thesis. His academic freedom to profess his thesis – his 'opinion' – is recognized, and the thesis is accepted and applauded for its originality, because it is the fruit of his own intellectual labour. Henceforth, the new doctor, the new professor of original ideas, is authorized to profess his opinions freely, unhindered by any extraneous force. This phenomenon of the doctorate's authority, the dignity of the doctoral degree, first came into being in classical Islam in the guilds for the study of the discipline of the Shariah (Divine Law).

Universities must produce graduates who not only excel in their own chosen field of specialization such as engineering, law, medicine and economics, but also have a firm grasp of dialectics and philosophy, in addition to having a taste for art, literature and music. Students must aspire to be multidimensional men of learning, *mutafannīn*, as they were called during the apogee of Islamic civilization. In fact, the Western idea of the Renaissance Man corresponds to the idea of the *mutafannun*, inasmuch as the *studia humanitatis* – the humanities – were none other than what the Muslims knew as the *adabiyyāt*, which included the study of grammar (*nahw*), rhetoric (*kataba*), poetry (*shiᶜr*), history (*akhbār* or *tārīkh*), epistemology (*maᶜrifa*) and moral philosophy (*ᶜilm al-akhlāq*).

For students to develop the love for philosophy and science and the taste for art, literature and music, they require an environment conducive to the pursuit of learning and intellectual ventilation. For this reason, libraries must be well-stocked with the canons of world literature, and records and commentaries of the major intellectual debates and disputes of all ages. For even in our time, raging polemics and controversial discourses continue to characterize a vibrant intellectual tradition. Virtually no discipline, be it jurisprudence, economic theory and policy, philosophy, philosophy of science, and the humanities in general, is exempt from that characteristic. It is pathetic if students and faculty do not participate in the discourses, content to being officious bystanders, satisfied merely to listen to the distant echoes. But it is tragic indeed if they are totally unaware of those intellectual battles.

Inevitably, the burden of establishing the intellectual and humanistic environment that we envisage falls on the intellectual community. They must exhibit mental vigour and intellectual fecundity; be thorough and competent in their chosen discipline, and at the same time, be a connoisseur of art, literature and music, having acquired the mental horizon of the *mutafannun* or the Renaissance Man. It is the mind and not the body which makes the man. Or in the words of the celebrated humanist Abu'l Fath al-Busti:

*Yā khādim al-jismi! kam tasqā bi-khidmatihi!*
*Li taṭluba 'l-ribḥa mimma fīhi khusrānu.*
*Aqbil ʿala 'l-nafsi wa 'stakmil faḍā'ilahā*
*Fa anta bi 'l-nafsi, lā bi 'l-jismi, insānu.*[13]

O Slave of the body! How you toil to serve it!
Where there's nothing but loss, you seek to profit.
Turn to the mind, which needs to be perfect:
You are a man, not by the body, but by the intellect.

## Endnotes

1   Said, Edward W., *Culture and Imperialism*, New York: Vintage, 1994, p. xxvi.

2   Arnold, Matthew, *Culture and Anarchy*, London: Chelsea House Publishers, 1983, p. 11.

3   Bloom, Harold, *The Western Canon*, Orlando: Harcourt Brace and Company, 1994, p. 531.

4   Hughes, Robert, *Culture of Complaint*, London: HarperCollins Publishers, 1994, p. 85.

5   De las Casas, Bartolomé, *A Short Account of the Destruction of the Indies*, edited and translated by Nigel Griffith, Middlesex: Penguin, 1992, p. 12.

6   Mill, John Stuart, *On Liberty*, in *Great Books of the World Vol. 40*, edited by Mortimer J. Adler, Chicago: Encyclopaedia Britannica, Inc., 1991, p. 272.

7   Alatas, Syed Hussein, *The Myth of the Lazy Native*, London: Frank Cass and Co. Ltd, 1977.

8   Hadith narrated by Tirmizi.

9   Rosenthal, Franz, *Knowledge Triumphant*, Leiden: E.J. Brill, 1970.

10  Al-Ghazali, Abu Hamid Muhammad bin Muhammad, *Ehya Ulum Al-Din*, Cairo: Dar Ehya Al-Kutub Al-Arabiah, undated, Chapter 1, p. 8.

11  Bloom, Allan, *The Closing of the American Mind*, New York: Simon and Schuster, 1987, Chapter 13, p. 346.

12 Iqbal, Muhammad, *The Secrets of the Self*, translation and notes by R.A. Nicholson, Lahore: Sh. Muhammad Ashraf, 1972.

13 *Muntazam*, VII, 73, cited as epigraph in George Makdisi, *The Rise of Humanism in Classical Islam and the Christian West*, Edinburgh: Edinburgh University Press, 1980.

# Islam in Southeast Asia

In his journey from China to the Levant in 1292, Marco Polo stayed for five months at a city port of northeast Sumatra called Perlak. He observed:

> that the people of Ferlec (sic) used all to be idolaters, but owing to contact with Saracen merchants, who continually resort here in their ships, they have all been converted to the law of Mahomet (sic). This applies only to the inhabitants of the city. The people of the mountains live like beasts.[1]

This early report of a Muslim community in the Malay archipelago provides a clue to the particular nuance of the region today. Islam came to Southeast Asia borne on the seas by sufis and merchants rather than overland by soldiers brandishing swords. Conversion was by choice, not coercion, beginning with the urban ruling class and the trading community. Historical accounts in the Malay and Javanese annals (*Sejarah Melayu* and *Babad Tanah Djawi*) record the interchangeability of roles between sufi mystics, preachers and traders in the course of the propagation of the religion. Thus, according to T.W. Arnold, in *The Preaching of Islam*:

> ... there is evidence enough to show the existence of peaceful missionary efforts to spread the faith of Islam during the last 600 years. Preaching and persuasion rather than force and violence have been the main characteristics of this missionary movement.[2]

This peaceful and gradual Islamization has moulded the Southeast Asian Muslim psyche into one which is cosmopolitan, open-minded, tolerant and amenable to cultural diversity. Of course, their outlook is also fashioned by the strong presence of people of other faiths who reciprocate Muslim tolerance. Unlike non-Muslims in the West, their perception of Islam is not distorted by the prism of the Crusades. The suggestion by Orientalist scholars that this mutual tolerance is because, in Southeast Asia, Islam is merely a "thin veneer" having no profound impact on the beliefs and practices of Muslims, has been largely debunked, although a superficial study of the *abangan* trait among the Javanese would render some truth to the argument. Nevertheless, as a prominent Muslim scholar, Professor Syed Muhammad Naquib al-Attas asserts, Islam transformed the "essential character and world view of the Malay-Javanese civilization" to one which is essentially "modern" – from a perspective based on magic, myth and superstition to that which is scientific and rational, in conformity with the spirit of the Quran.[3]

Almost without exception, Muslim nations have experienced colonialism. Many have not quite fully recovered from its traumatic after-effects, as manifested in extreme attitudes towards the West. There are those who blame the West and invoke the Western bogey for every conceivable failing of their own. And while antipathy towards the West may have been justified in the immediate post-colonial years, there is no reasonable excuse for the persistence of such an attitude. At the other extreme are the culturally dispossessed elite classes, who remain spellbound and enchanted with the West. While Southeast Asian Muslims are not altogether immune to these internal tensions, they have neither allowed them to paralyse nation-building nor to poison their relations with the rest of the world. Instead of nursing bitterness about the past, they choose the path of magnanimity, which reflects the essential Malay character. The Filipino patriot José Rizal has given us a glimpse of this Southeast Asian trait. He wrote:

> The Filipino ... remembers only the kindness he has received; he easily forgets resentments, and if he has only smiles and tears for those who have treated him harshly when he sees them depart, what would he have for one who had been good when he sees him in misfortune?[4]

By being moderate and pragmatic, Southeast Asian Muslims are neither compromising the teachings and ideals of Islam nor pandering to the whims and fancies of the times. On the contrary, such an approach is necessary to realize the societal ideals of Islam such as justice, equitable distribution of wealth, fundamental rights and liberties. This approach is sanctioned in a saying of the Prophet of Islam, to the effect that "the best way to conduct your affairs is to choose the middle path."[5]

This principle of *awsaṭuhā* – the middle path – which corresponds to the Confucian *chun yung* and the golden mean of Aristotelian ethics, reinforces the moderate elements in the Southeast Asian Muslim character and shapes the understanding and practice of Islam. This moderation leads to a pragmatic approach in social, economic and political life. True, Southeast Asian Muslims are not without their share of problems. But what differentiates them from their brethren in other parts of the world is their sense of priorities.

The proponents of the imposition of Muslim laws or the establishment of an Islamic state are confined to the periphery. Southeast Asian Muslims prefer to concentrate on the task of ensuring economic growth and eradicating poverty, instead of amputating the limbs of thieves. They would rather strive to improve the welfare of the women and children in their midst, than spend their days elaborately defining the nature and institutions of the ideal Islamic State. They do not believe it would make one less of a Muslim to promote economic growth, to master the information revolution, and to demand justice for women. Nor do they believe it would strengthen one's commitment to religion by instilling anxiety among people of other faiths.

Moderation and pragmatism warrant that extreme emotions be kept under tight rein. Whilst recognizing the legitimate rights of victims of oppression and persecution to use whatever means available to liberate themselves, the head must rule the heart, and passion must give way to sobriety. For if it were otherwise, it will be a sure-fire formula for violence and destruction. Reason and common sense must prevail in order for us to view things in the proper perspective and set our priorities right.

A major predicament of Muslims is the failure to come to terms with present-day realities. It should be recognized that the causes of general confusion and malaise of the Muslims are rooted in history. Islamic civilization, after all, is only just "recovering" after a long period of decline. With the fall in 1492 of the Muslim kingdom of Granada to the *reconquista* of Ferdinand of Aragon and Isabella of Castille, Islamic civilization was severed from Europe, where it had established itself during the preceding eight centuries as an integral part of that continent. The Islamic world took its own course of development, quite oblivious to the gigantic enterprise of the Renaissance and the Enlightenment, and degenerated into complacency. Islamic arts and humanities did not gain fresh impetus from the rise of the powerful intellectual venture ushered in by Humanism in Europe. The decline in the sciences accelerated into decay and Muslim scholars became almost ignorant of the new cosmology initiated by the Copernican Revolution. Thus, in its subsequent development, Islamic civilization had very little influence, if at all, in the emerging "modern" civilization.

While European power immediately radiated from the Iberian peninsula westwards across the Atlantic, and eastwards via the horn of Africa to the Malay archipelago, Muslim civilization, which had hitherto stood at the centre of the world, was gradually consigned to the margins. No doubt, the new civilization of the Moghuls was to rise in India and bequeath to the world miraculous works of art in the fields of architecture and music. The full flowering of the Ottoman Turks was only beginning. At its height, the Ottoman empire was to hold sway even to the very gates of Vienna until the last century. Indeed, the grandeur of the Ottoman Empire was the least known and acknowledged among world empires. In terms of size and population under its control, it was greater than the dominions of Alexander the Great or Genghis Khan at the height of their respective powers. And no united empire had ever survived intact for as long as it did – 600 years of uninterrupted rule.

Yet, despite their grand achievements, both the Moghuls and the Ottomans were to be mere peripheral powers in the emerging world system. They were never partners in the construction of the modern age. Sulayman the Magnificent reportedly said, "Whoever controls the sea controls the world." He was among the first to foresee the new age of maritime power. But the Ottoman defeat in the decisive naval Battle of Lepanto in 1571 soon ended whatever hope there was to redeem the inglorious exit of Islam from Spain. Later, the Muslims painfully witnessed the gap in technological strength upon the first encounter with a modern European power when Napoleon set foot in Egypt in 1798, triggering the forward movement of European domination of the Muslim world.

## KNOWLEDGE TRIUMPHANT

Islamic civilization is, to borrow Franz Rosenthal's phrase, "knowledge triumphant" and thus the ulema have a central role in the realm of scholarship and are a moral force within society. In the Southeast Asian experience, even with the decline and decay of statecraft, the sheer moral authority of the ulema has exerted tremendous influence. This has enabled the preservation of equilibrium among contending forces, so that Muslim societies in the region generally manifest justice, orderliness and compassion. During the colonial period, the tradition of learning continued unabated, and many ulema figured prominently in the struggles for independence from European rule of their homeland. Southeast Asians formed a significant part of the intellectual community in Mecca at the turn of the century, involving themselves not only in matters which related to their native lands but also in issues which affected the Muslim *umma* as a whole. Amir Shakib Arsalan's *Our Decline and Its Causes*, a book which enjoyed wide circulation throughout the Muslim world at the time and had tremendous influence in the on-going pan-Islamic anti-imperialist movement, was written in response to a challenge raised by Sheikh Muhammad Bashuni Imran of Borneo in a letter to the editor of the Egyptian journal *al-Manār*.

While Islam was progressively marginalized in world history, a similar process of intellectual decline and decay was gradually setting in. With the deterioration in economic activities over centuries of colonial subjugation, poverty and destitution began to surface in Muslim societies. Patronage of learning, arts and sciences suffered. As the level of learning declined, superstitions grew. The general public could no longer be counted upon to participate intelligently in societal processes as responsible and enlightened citizens. Among the ulema, conservatism and rigidity began to take root in the face of external challenges and internal decadence. The doctrine of *taqlīd* (uncritical imitation) was instituted. Innovation, change and inquiry became suspect. In such a climate, the ulema became isolated from the practical aspects of everyday life as they devoted themselves almost entirely to the issue of *fiqh* (jurisprudence) and limited study and commentary of the works of the great scholars of the classical era. Serious problems which cried for urgent attention, including poverty, illiteracy and other forms of social malaise, were ignored. Islamic scholarship was confined to textual studies of language, traditions and orthodox jurisprudence. It became absorbed, not in the urgent task of championing the broad vision and civilizational ideals of Islam in the face of the onslaught of modern secular ideologies, but in attempting to unearth past solutions to resolve sometimes petty issues. Fazlur Rahman laments that while steady encroachments were being made upon the Shariah (Divine Law), not only by state-made law but also by the customary law of different cultural regions, the ulema "clung tenaciously" to two segments of the Shariah: the "five pillars" of Islam, the "minimal Islam", and the *ḥudūd*, the "negative or punitive Islam" when "the integral teaching of the Quran and the historic struggle of the Prophet that provided the socio-moral context for these provisions ... had already been lost sight of."[6]

The effort to revive the spirit of inquiry and reasoned discourse (*tajdīd*) required no less than a thorough transformation of mental outlook. To regain their central position in society, the ulema need to manifest intellectual vigour and societal relevance. They have to compete among the multifarious contending forces for the hearts and minds of the people. If a disproportionate number of ulema were to devote themselves entirely to jurisprudence, the other sciences and arts would be bereft of moral leadership. The issue of penal sanctions of the Shariah, for example, is a preoccupation of the majority of the ulema, although mass poverty is more pervasive than criminality, and the suffering of the destitute and the hungry in so many parts of the Muslim world demands greater attention and compassion.

In general, Muslims have yet to respond fully to the call by Jamaluddin al-Afghani more than 100 years ago to master scientific knowledge to enable them to advance technologically and economically. In a lecture at Calcutta in 1882, the initiator of the pan-Islamic movement asserted that it was science that had given the power to European imperialists to subjugate the Muslims:

> The Europeans have now put their hands on every part of the world. The English have reached Afghanistan; the French have seized Tunisia. In reality, this usurpation, aggression and conquest has not come from the French or the English. Rather it is science that everywhere manifests its greatness and power.[7]

Muslims need to address urgent social and economic issues such as the eradication of poverty and illiteracy, the provision of employment, decent housing and other social amenities. These are preconditions before certain specific Shariah injunctions can be translated into legislation. Indeed, the construction of an outer edifice of Islamic governance without the true substance of physical and spiritual well-being of the *umma* would be a travesty of the *maqāṣid al-Sharīᶜa*, the ideals and objectives of religion itself. It is tantamount to insisting on a form of religion devoid of substance.

Until recently, the theory of *maqāṣid al-Sharīᶜa*, formulated around six centuries ago by the jurist Ibrahim ibn Musa al-Shatibi in his *al-Muwāfaqāt* had been relegated to obscurity. In essence, his jurisprudence entails attaching priority to the promotion of the humanitarian and compassionate values of Islam which are of universal and perpetual significance, as opposed to the literalism and legalism of mainstream Islamic jurisprudence. The latter effectively portrays Islam as a static religion which has lost its relevance. Ulema such as Muhammad ibn Ashur, Sheikh Yusuf al-Qaradhawi and the late Sheikh Muhammad al-Ghazali, however, have taken the lead in expounding al-Shatibi's approach from a background of traditional Islamic scholarship. Sheikh al-Qaradhawi particularly is an advocate of the *fiqh al-awlawiyyāt*, the understanding of priorities, as a juristic basis for social policies. Under this approach, which appears to be gaining acceptance among the mainstream ulema of Southeast Asia, the application of the *ḥudūd*, fixed punishments prescribed by the Quran and the Traditions of the Prophet of Islam for certain offences, is not necessarily among the top priorities of contemporary Muslim societies.

The painful political convulsions of most Muslim countries under colonial rule did not end with independence. There was great hope for a new beginning, but after successive failures, cynicism supplanted hope. Independence promised much but delivered little. The mistake was to seek total change and establish a new utopia. Dissent and alternative views of nation building were crushed or summarily dismissed. In some cases, the new regimes surpassed their erstwhile colonial masters in political repression. Yet, in Southeast Asia, the frenzy of post-colonial rhetoric was replaced by a more down-to-earth and pragmatic approach. The Indonesians courted radical ideology for a while during the early post-colonial period, but pragmatism eventually won the day. Successive Muslim leaders in Malaysia have always emphasized economic and social development through a *modus vivendi* with the non-Muslim minority in the country. The education of all children, Muslim and non-Muslim, is always accorded the highest priority in the allocation of the nation's resources. Nowhere in the contemporary Muslim world has there been a greater emphasis on the education of children of both sexes than in Southeast Asia. In addition to government-funded schools, Islamic social and religious organizations undertake massive educational programmes for boys and girls. The scale of the efforts by the Muhammadiyah and Nahdatul Ulama in Indonesia, for example, is quite unprecedented elsewhere in the Muslim world, surpassing the number of educational institutions in Arab and African countries.

There have been many instances in the recent past which demonstrate the Muslims' collective impotence in international affairs. Despite their numerical strength and control of strategic resources, their views are unsolicited and their protestations ignored, in Bosnia-Herzegovina, Iraq and other flashpoints. The absence of credible initiatives in international affairs by Muslim countries is a reflection of the lack of will and determination to uplift the people from their present deplorable state. At present, not less than 1.2 billion people in the developing world are surviving under conditions of abject poverty, with more than half of them living in Muslim countries. Unless drastic measures are taken, the number of Muslims trapped in poverty and destitution would increase by the millions in the coming years. In Sub-Saharan Africa, the picture is particularly depressing. In 1985, there were already 184 million poor. In 1990, there were 216 million. And in the year 2000, 304 million people are expected to be in poverty.

These problems are not insurmountable. In East Asia, for instance, the number of poor people has dropped from 182 million in 1985 to 169 million in 1990, and is expected to fall to about 73 million in the year 2000. The real challenge facing

Muslims today is to break away from the stifling and debilitating confines of ideological conflicts and stagnant economies towards the path of growth and development. Only through growth can equity be assured.

Growth cannot be sustained in an economy that is not conducive to trade, investment, entrepreneurship and risk-taking. It is essential that Muslim countries embark upon a policy of economic reform or liberalization, despite the fear in some quarters that the Muslims would become less Islamic by shifting their focus towards economics.

The late Ismail al-Faruqi, in his essay, "Is the Muslim Definable in Terms of His Economic Pursuits?", has refuted the claim that there was any inherent contradiction between Islam and the continuous struggle to improve economic well-being. His vision of development was certainly not based on the idea of *homo economicus*, the one-dimensional model with an obsession with economics alone. He thought in terms of *homo islamicus*, a concept that demands a balanced emphasis on material and spiritual well-being. The economic imperative of development is equally borne out by the fact that some of the ideals of Islam such as justice, the pursuit of knowledge, and the promotion of the arts and culture, can only be realized within the context of economic prosperity. Sectarian conflicts, ideological struggle and petty politics in recent years have left the Muslims poorer in every sense of the word, making them the bugbear of the global community.

In many Muslim countries, attempts to increase the wealth of the people must take into account particular features of the economy. For instance, landlordism and monopolistic practices are stumbling blocks to the upliftment of the poor and downtrodden. In such cases, land reform, agricultural modernization and economic diversification are imperative. As the resistance to change will be enormous, political courage is essential.

The future of the Muslims will be determined more by careful planning and concrete action than by the beauty of conceptual formulation or the fervour of moral exhortation. Muslim institutions of learning must be in the forefront in the advocacy of social and economic reforms throughout the Muslim world. Many Muslim intellectuals have been content to abandon the centre stage of worldly action, preferring instead the comfort of the moral high ground. In their striving to remain unsullied by the often sordid realities of worldly affairs, they deprive the people of leadership in a very challenging and competitive world. On the other hand, there are also those who choose to plunge into the arena without the breadth of vision to realize that we live in a very diverse, multicultural, multi-ethnic and fragmented universe.

The Southeast Asian region has been often cited as a case where Muslims have come to terms with modernity. Their less illustrious history could be the explanation. Throughout history, Southeast Asian Islam has remained on the margins, even as the number of its adherents swells to surpass that of the Arabs, Turks and Persians. But this lack of historic greatness is a boon. The Arabs, Turks or Persians are weighed down by the millstone of greatness. On the other hand, the Malays are less haunted by the ghost of the past, more attentive to present realities, and have greater awareness of their many shades and nuances. No doubt, the arrival of Islam in the Malay world about seven centuries ago had ushered in a new period. Yet, the most successful Malay-Muslim kingdom before the advent of European colonialism, the Malaccan maritime kingdom, a city which Tomé Pires described in his *Suma Oriental* as "... made for merchandise, fitter than any other in the world ... to which trade and commerce between the different nations for a thousands leagues must come ... in (which) very often 84 languages have been found spoken, everyone distinct", rose and fell within barely a century.[8] Intellectual and philosophical creativity in the Malay world reached its height only in the seventeenth century in Acheh, in the works of Hamzah Fansuri and Nuruddin al-Raniri. Towards the turn of the last century, there was the figure of Raja Ali Haji, who had tremendous influence in subjects ranging from theology and history to language. None of these figures, however, could be ranked with the great scholars and interpreters of Islam from among the Arabs and Persians.

The culture of tolerance is the hallmark of Southeast Asian Islam. When a band of Muslim fanatics went around desecrating Hindu temples in Malaysia 20 years ago, the chorus of Muslim condemnation was unequivocal. The full force of the law was brought to bear upon the perpetrators. Such violent outbursts are the work of deviants who have no place in any society which professes to uphold the moral teachings of any religion. Thus, extremism in all its forms must be wholly repudiated. But tolerance cannot be demanded from one community only. It has to be mutual. That is why reports of the destruction of mosques and Muslim holy places in other countries are received with shock and despair in Southeast Asia. A plural, multi-religious society is living perpetually on the brink of catastrophe. Relations between Muslims and non-Muslims must be governed by moral and ethical considerations. The seeds of militancy are everywhere and each community must ensure that they will not germinate and multiply through discontent and alienation. So, participation and social justice is fundamental in Southeast Asia in the age of the nation-state.

Southeast Asians will not forget that since time immemorial, their region has been the theatre where the great civilizations have crossed paths. But they are honest enough to know that the region is not a great melting pot. The collective memory of each community is as strong as ever and each holds dearly to its identity. Yet, Southeast Asia today is moving towards greater cohesiveness, and a sense of community could not be fostered without shared values. The Indonesian motto, *Bhinneka Tunggal Ika* (Unity in Diversity) defines the region culturally. The challenge to Muslims and the people of other confessions is to effectively articulate their moral vision and intensify the search for common ethical ground. The people of various faiths in Southeast Asia are proceeding beyond mere tolerance. Together, they will eventually have to confront the stark realities in their midst: corruption, authoritarianism, modern feudalism and injustices in many shades and guises. Only moral fortitude will give them the courage of conviction to battle these iniquities.

The wave of Islamic revivalism that began with the anti-imperialist struggles of the previous century has gained further momentum in our time among Muslims in Southeast Asia. The energy potential must be properly directed so as not to deteriorate or be corrupted into blind fanaticism which could precipitate into violent clashes with other cultures. There are indeed signs, however, that these religious energies, aligned with forces of social conservatism, have served to marginalize the Muslims in the rapidly changing world. Thus, we need to reassert the universalism of Islam, its values of justice, compassion and tolerance in a world that is yearning for a sense of direction and for genuine peace. If this could be achieved, Muslims can truly contribute to the shaping of a new world.

## Endnotes

1 Polo, Marco, *The Travels of Marco Polo*, London: Penguin Books, 1958, p. 253.

2 Arnold, T.W., *The Preaching of Islam*, Delhi: Renaissance Publishing House, 1984, p. 363.

3 Al-Attas, Syed Muhammad Naquib, *Islam and Secularism*, Kuala Lumpur: ISTAC, 1993.

4 Rizal, José in a letter to Mariano Rincon, 11 August 1885, in *Miscellaneous Correspondence of Dr. José Rizal*, translated by Encarnacion Alzona, Manila: National Historical Institute, 1992, p. 67.

5 Hadith narrated by al-Baihaqi.

6 Rahman, Fazlur, *Islam and Modernity*, Chicago: University of Chicago Press, 1982, p. 31.

7 Keddie, Nikki R., *An Islamic Response to Imperialism. Political and Religious Writings of Sayyid Jamal ad-Din al-Afghani*, Berkeley: University of California Press, 1983, pp. 102–103.

8 Cortesao, Armado (trans.), *The Suma Oriental of Tomé Pires: An Account of the East from the Red Sea to Japan, Written in Malacca and India in 1512–1515*, 2 Vols., London: Hakluyt Society, 1944, pp. 286–287.

# The Asia of the Future

If you can look into the seeds of time,
And say which grain will grow and which will not
Speak then to me.[1]

The future is embedded in time present. Yet, its shape and character is a matter of conjecture. With the benefit of hindsight, we seek to explain events that were previously unforeseen. It was only after the collapse of the Berlin Wall and the disintegration of the Soviet Empire in 1989 that we began to see how ideas and events had been converging for decades.

For a very long time, Asia was incomprehensible. It was a metaphor for the nebulous and the mysterious. To the Irish poet W.B. Yeats, the Asiatic essence was its "vague immensities". Asia baffled its observers and strained their capacity to the limit in conceptualizing and organizing meaning. Unlike the West, Asia does not have its defining moments in history, and a common stock of ideas that moulds a shared outlook and conscious identification with a common civilization. There was no Hellenic Age, no Dark Ages, and no French Revolution. Unlike the West, which has

Christianity, Asia has no single religion. There was no Enlightenment, as in Europe in the eighteenth century, to spawn a cluster of ideas and common attitudes towards life, the individual and society.

These are the basic complexities which render the task of foretelling the future of Asia a very dicey affair. It would be easy to speculate on the future of China or India or Japan or even a grouping such as Southeast Asia. One is on even firmer ground when dealing with individual Asian traditions such as Confucianism, Hinduism or Islam. But when there is no consensus on the identity of the subject whose future we are divining, we are shooting in the dark.

Nevertheless, this difficulty in pinning down the common character of Asia is not absolute and permanent. It is being exaggerated by the West, which takes for granted its identity as if it were bestowed on it almost overnight by virtue of some all-encompassing monolithic process. But no one can really say when the West became the West as it is today. That sense of common identity and consciousness of belonging to a distinct culture and tradition is hardly more than 200 years old, perhaps even less. It is a sense of identity moulded by the ideals of its own civilization. Yet, the West's understanding of itself is no less shaped by its relations with others, and its sense of having something unique and benevolent to disseminate to others. Joseph Conrad captures this feeling in sardonic and incisive terms in *The Heart of Darkness*:

> The conquest of the earth, which mostly means the taking it away from those who have a different complexion or slightly flatter noses than ourselves, is not a pretty thing when you look into it too much. What redeems it is the idea only. An idea at the back of it; not a sentimental pretence but an idea; and an unselfish belief in the idea – something you can set up, and bow down before, and offer a sacrifice to ..."[2]

The West has expressed its identity. Its ideals and moral values have been articulated fully. There is little dispute of its own self-image and in that sense, it may have reached the end of history. But Asia has no settled identity as yet. It is in the process of coming into being. The long and intense process of self-definition and self-understanding is just beginning.

The present revitalization of Asia is a continuation of the rejuvenation and reform movements which surfaced in the late nineteenth century all over the continent. Although those movements were primarily political in appearance and impact, especially when the various struggles for national liberation reached their height, their cultural and intellectual dimensions were equally remarkable and enduring. The project was captured by poet-philosopher Muhammed Iqbal in his *Zabur-e* *cAjam*:

> design a new temper
> of this country, and this age;
> create a new-born spirit;
> In this body grown too old.[3]

Asians today owe a profound debt to the early Asian nationalist movements, although they have reason to be critical of some of their developments in the post-colonial era. Their strident anti-Western rhetoric led to tensions and conflicts. In many instances, the slogans of liberation rang hollow because the people were made to suffer at the hands of incompetent and corrupt regimes. While the economic stagnation of some Asian countries, and even decay in a few, may be blamed on the colonial legacy and the inequitable international economic order, it nevertheless stands as an indictment of their misguided policies.

If the new wave of Asian resurgence is to contribute to global civilization it has, above all, to be benign in its effects. Asia suffered as a victim of the West in the latter's pursuit of wealth, power and domination, often disguising itself as an "emissary of pity and science and progress." As Asia gains wealth and power, it must search its deepest conscience. It should not now assume the role of the new executioner to replay the old history of oppression and injustice. Wealth undoubtedly will bring power. Lest one forget, the prophet of capitalism, Adam Smith, reminded us that wealth and power is the most universal cause of the corruption of our moral sentiments. Thus, genuine revival must also be a moral renewal. Asia must not look at the world from the perspective of power relations. The Atlantic community too must also not see Asia as a competitor to its ambition for global domination and fall prey to self-induced fear and insecurity.

Nothing is more visible in the rise of Asia than the economic aspect. Projections of growth to the middle of the next century have been anything but pessimistic. But the realization of these rosy forecasts is contingent upon the vicissitudes of national life, regional political dynamics and global peace. The rising tide of economic nationalism in the West, whether expressed in the rancid rhetoric of protectionism or cloaked in seemingly altruistic motives such as concern for civil liberties, the environment or workers' rights, poses a grave threat to Asia's attempts to unshackle itself from the chains of poverty. There are already indications that supranational institutions such as the World Trade Organization, in whose arenas many of these trade conflicts will be arbitrated, are more likely to be manipulated to support the claims of the rich and powerful than address the legitimate grievances of the developing countries.

Asian economic growth is dependent, as well, on the ability of the continent to keep pace with the global shift to a new economic structure powered by brains rather than brawn. For while the manufacturing sector will continue to be important, the new stimulus for growth will come from services and information-based industries. Information technology, growing exponentially, will, if properly utilized, provide a quantum leap into the twenty-first century economy. This will require not just a change in the mindset, but also massive investment by the public and private sectors in research and development, training and in the tools of high-technology. With the exception of Japan, general expenditure on research and development by Asian nations is still minimal. Much of the continent continues to rely on low-wage, low-technology areas for economic growth, while the value-added creative input is imported from the West. The rising cost of such intellectual property may soon negate whatever advantages in wage structures or raw materials that Asia has to offer. Thus, the role of education and human resources development will be crucial as Asia strives to develop an indigenous scientific and technological culture, as will the rearrangement of current societal configurations modelled on the hierarchical nature of the industrial age. Asia needs to undergo a paradigm shift as it seeks to respond to the utilitarian demands of the future without forsaking its identity, a challenge which requires a revitalization of Asia's traditions.

The construction of a just and realistic security arrangement is one of the greatest challenges not only to Asia but also to the world. Despite the end of the Cold War, the arms race continues unabated. The so-called "peace dividend" has fallen prey to the pursuit of new strategic alliances founded on narrow self-interests, which have replaced the ideological divides of old. Within the single decade of 1984 to 1994, the East Asian share of world military spending has doubled. The substantial reduction of military expenditure by safeguarding regional security through strategic military-defence arrangements will allow Asian nations to devote their resources primarily to economic and social programmes. Flashpoints are there, but military adventurism would be a less attractive option if the interest of the would-be perpetrator is deeply entangled and intertwined with the interest of the rest, which lies in peace and stability of the region through collaborative and synergistic economic relations. The way forward has been demonstrated in the tumultuous 1960s, when countries in Southeast Asia decided to form Asean and the establishment, in fact if not in name, of the East Asian Economic Caucus (EAEC), groupings in which nations, going beyond platitudes, willingly enter into arrangements of joint-sovereignty to generate investment in the region, including the marginalized areas. The proof that this concept is not only viable, but necessary, is already clear in the setting up of sub-subregional initiatives such as the Mekong Basin development plan to help the economies of Vietnam, Laos and Cambodia, and the railway project from Singapore to Kunming.

There are today in Asia progressive currents, yet, retrogressive countercurrents are not to be discounted. There are ardent advocates of democracy and civil society but there are also reactionary elements. The contest between the two forces is one of the great themes of Asia today and will remain so in many decades to come. If democracy is about the exercise of informed choice, then the information revolution is likely to be a friend of democracy, for an informed citizenry is also a responsible citizenry. The Internet, for example, offers us a new paradigm for the spread and accessibility of information, the lifeblood of a functioning democracy. The issues of privacy and individual freedom raised by the interactive value of the Internet are genuine problems for which a collective solution must be found. The answer, however, does not lie in censoring the medium. The best form of censorship is moral fortification, and this begins at home. Simply closing the doors will not only hurt our nations but push Asia back in the race for growth and prosperity.

However, mastery of the tools of information technology by itself is not enough. Even more crucial is the content of the information that is disseminated through the electronic channels of this new age. The creative energies of Asia, for long smothered by foreign colonial masters or home-grown despots, must be allowed to flourish if the continent is to play an active role in moulding the pivotal ideas of the new millennium.

The logic of economic growth will promote a regional and global outlook, yet, the revival of the consciousness of ethnic superiority and jingoistic nationalism will not only foster inward-looking attitudes but also supply the ideology for military adventurism. Even though the information revolution is an enemy to feudalism, authoritarianism, parochialism and ethnic chauvinism, the remnants of these are not going to meekly wither away, and instead, may acquire new forms and new vigour, and spread like a virulent disease, particularly if there is inequity and injustice. Democracy too, on the other hand, can be abused by a vocal and disruptive minority to the detriment of the larger community. Thus, democracy alone cannot be the panacea for the ills of Asia as we know them.

There appears to be collective amnesia on the part of the West about their history of democratization. Just as much as Rome was not built in a day, democracy in the West did not come about overnight. In fact, it took 450 years from Magna Carta's assertion of rights to the revolution of 1688 that ushered in the era of parliamentary supremacy.[4] Abraham Lincoln, "the Great Emancipator" of the United States, suspended the writ of *habeas corpus* in 1862, a matter Lincoln thought "so routine" that he did not even mention it to his Cabinet. Thus, the issue is not whether a nation is "democratic" or whether it is moving fast enough towards democracy, but rather, whether democracy results in humane governance which is the ultimate test of civil society. In such a society, the people's legitimate expectations are met and their rights and liberties safeguarded. Only the fostering of a genuine civil society, of which democracy is a crucial component, can assure the path of sustained growth – economically, socially and politically.

The collective management of regional affairs will be as important as that of the domestic concerns of each country because of the scope and nature of the problems that we face. Intra-regional cooperation will help nations deal with critical issues more effectively than if they were to try to resolve them on their own. Isolationism is and ought to remain a thing of the past. Thus, the trend towards regionalism is both beneficial and inevitable. Unlike the past, where regionalism was often motivated by a quest for dominance, this new era will see a regionalism based on the need for mutual benefit. Cooperation and trust can be expected to replace conflict and mistrust. The private sector is already weaving a web of interconnectivity that governments are seeking to emulate under this concept of "open regionalism". Regional institutions, both governmental and non-governmental, will mushroom. Governments will endeavour to coordinate activities on a regional scale and the people will also have a life of their own. Ideas, views and voices will compete like products in the market-place. Governments will collaborate for mutual interest, as will workers, artists and nature lovers, just a few of the pan-regional groups that will certainly emerge.

Manufacturers will have their own lobbyists or non-profit institutes working for their benefit. Asian societies and governments have acquired a fondness for the free market of goods and services. But increasingly, they will have to deal with the free market of ideas. Some will vehemently oppose this Babel, even though the alternative is a sterile and sanitized uniformity. Or worse, it will be a return to the age of ideological rectitude, preceded by historical amnesia and a replay of the monstrosities of the Cambodian killing fields.

At a deeper level, Asia will have to come to grips with problems that are primarily cultural. The search for cultural solidarity, common meaning and sense of connectedness will be a challenge that demands intense energy of the mind and fertility of imagination. It also requires that Asia fully regains its self-confidence, but this confidence should not be allowed to degenerate into arrogance. To quote Lao-tze, "He who can overcome others is strong; but he who can overcome himself is mighty." Asian unity has become an idea very much scorned. First, such aversion has political roots. The prospect of the immense continent with the greatest economic potential coming together seems not only intolerable but dangerous. The Afro-Asian unity exemplified in Bandung in 1955 was a nightmare to the Cold Warriors and they would not allow its spectre to walk the earth again. Secondly, the mind which has been conditioned by the idea of a "melting pot" will understandably find it difficult to countenance the concept of *Bhinneka Tunggal Ika* (Unity in Diversity), where multiculturality is regarded not as a passing fad but as a way of life ingrained among peoples of varied ethnic origins practising their own religious faiths but interacting and enriching the great civilizations which call Asia home. Inclusivism is a strong tendency in the Asian mind. This is not a superficial attitude acquired only after the encounter with multiculturalism now in vogue in the West. Centuries ago, Muslim thinkers conceived and expounded the concept of *al-waḥda fi 'l-kathrā*, which presupposes the essential oneness and transcendent connectedness of the apparent diversity on the surface. Asians, firmly rooted in their cultural and spiritual traditions, do possess the intellectual capacity to perceive the cultural unity of Asia, its meta-culture. Thus, if we continue to exhibit an economic vibrancy and growth based on balanced and holistic development, that is, the concept of development guided by ethical and social concern, by the middle of the next century, this sense of unity is likely to deepen and become more pervasive.

## NEW ORDER

A combination of Asean cohesiveness, East Asian economic strength, and developing countries' solidarity through the Non-Aligned Movement and similar groupings should give us the firmness and confidence to influence the course of world events. Nevertheless, the making of a new order cannot be a question of strength or might alone, be it economic, political or military. This is because an order founded on strength or might will only mean servility of the weak to the strong or dependence of the poor on the rich. What we need is a new pattern of relationships where the use of power and influence is guided by ethical considerations, and where assistance does not breed dependence.

In our own small way, we have striven to realize these ideals in Asean. Asean succeeded so well because the Asean Pax was established without an imperium. The sense of equality and mutual respect is deeply entrenched. Should any country venture to dominate others the grouping would collapse immediately as was the case with several other regional groupings in the developing world. Collectively, we strive to achieve true and lasting peace, not a dry and frigid accord founded on balances of power and deterrence, of checks and counterchecks.

The new world order cannot be based on the hegemony or insular perspective of a particular civilization and culture. The notion of a clash of civilizations is the latest manifestation that the

West has limited ability to deal with a pluralistic and multicultural world. The probable reassuring development is that it is in the domain of ideas and knowledge that the course of events in the political sphere has often been foretold. More than a decade before the revolt of the masses against it, socialism had lost its appeal among intellectuals. Now, in the market-place of ideas, the totalitarian concept of modernity, which is the philosophical foundation for the European and Atlantic claim for hegemony, is helpless under constant intellectual assault from multiculturalism and postmodernism. In the history of civilizations, once the ideational foundation of a civilization is undermined, its fate is sealed. Thus, the proliferation of writing debunking modernity and advocating multiculturalism, including its many artistic expressions, indicates that a new pattern of relations, with its political ramifications, is fast emerging.

The new global order must be rooted in the reality of a pluralistic and multicultural world. The rise of the West since the Renaissance and the Enlightenment has contributed immensely to the store of human culture and learning. Despite the harm the Western powers had inflicted during and after colonialism, no non-Western society can deny its indebtedness to the West. We have absorbed from the West not only their science and technology, but also the modern education system, statecraft and economic management. But we cannot be slavish in our adoption. While we must continuously strive to realize noble ideals such as democracy, human freedom and dignity, we cannot turn a blind eye to the realities in our society. We cannot accept that all those who clamour for democracy and freedom are well-intentioned. Just as the devil can cite scripture for his own purpose, the most totalitarian regimes can also trumpet slogans about liberty, equality and freedom in order to foment hatred and create disorder. The threat of ethnic fanaticism and religious extremism is very real. It is this complexity of the situation the Western observers and even governments fail to appreciate. As the Mexican Nobel laureate Octavio Paz has said, the West does not seem to be wanting in good intentions, but it suffers from lack of humanity.

As Asia's reawakening proceeds apace, both East and West should forge a symbiosis of cultures and realize the universal community of the human race. In the words of Tagore:

> The night has ended.
> Put out the light of the lamp of thine own narrow corner smudged with smoke.
> The great morning which is for all appears in the East.
> Let its light reveal us to each other who walk on the same path of pilgrimage.[5]

Endnotes

1 Shakespeare, *Macbeth*, Act I, scene iii.

2 Conrad, Joseph, *The Heart of Darkness*, London: Penguin, 1994, p. 10.

3 Iqbal, Muhammad, *Zabur-e ᶜAjam (Persian Psalms)*, translated by A.J. Arberry, Lahore: Sh. Muhammad Ashraf, 1948.

4 Barber, Benjamin R., *Jihad vs. McWorld*, New York: Times Books, 1995.

5 Dutta, Krishna, and Robinson, Andrew, *Rabindranath Tagore: The Myriad-Minded Man*, New York: St. Martin's Press, 1995, p. 317.

# Select Bibliography

Al-Attas, Syed Muhammad Naquib, *Islam and Secularism*, Kuala Lumpur: ISTAC, 1993.

Al-Attas, Syed Muhammad Naquib, *Prolegomena to the Metaphysics of Islam*, Kuala Lumpur: ISTAC, 1995.

Al-Faruqi, Ismail R. and Al-Faruqi, Lois Lamya, *The Cultural Atlas of Islam*, New York: Macmillan Publishing Company, 1986.

Al-Ghazali, *Ihya Ulumiddin*, 8 Vols., Jakarta: Percetakan Menara Kudus, 1980.

Al-Qaradawi, Yusof, *Priorities of the Islamic Movement in the Coming Phase*, Cairo: Dar Al-Nashr, 1992.

Alatas, Syed Hussein, *The Myth of the Lazy Native*, London: Frank Cass and Co. Ltd, 1977.

Alatas, Syed Hussein, *The Problem of Corruption*, Singapore: Times Books International, 1989.

Alisjahbana, Sutan Takdir, *Indonesia: Social and Cultural Revolution*, London: Oxford University Press, 1966.

Alwani, Taha Jabir Fayyad, *Ethics of Disagreement in Islam*, prepared from the original Arabic by Abdul Wahid Hamid; edited by A.S. Shaikh Ali, Herndon: The International Institute of Islamic Thought, 1993.

Armesto, Felipe Fernandez, *Millenium – A History of the Last Thousand Years*, New York: Charles Scribner's Sons, 1995.

Arnold, Matthew, *Culture and Anarchy*, London: Chelsea House Publishers, 1983.

Asad, Muhammad, *The Principles of State and Government in Islam*, Gibraltar: Dar Al-Andalus Ltd, 1981.

Blacker, Carmen, *The Japanese Enlightenment: A Study of the Writings of Fukuzama Yukichi*, Cambridge: Cambridge Univeristy Press, 1964.

Bellah, Robert N. *et. al.*, *Habits of the Heart*, Berkeley: University of California Press, 1985.

Bewkey, Aisha Abdurrahman (trans.), *Al-Muwatta of Imam Malik ibn Anas*, London: Kegan Paul International, 1989.

Blinder, Alan S., *Hard Heads, Soft Hearts*, Massachusetts: Addison-Wesley Publishing Co, Inc., 1987.

Bloom, Allan, *The Closing of the American Mind*, New York: Simon and Schuster, 1987.

Bloom, Harold, *The Western Canon*, Orlando: Harcourt Brace and Company, 1994.

Braudel, Fernand, *A History of Civilizations*, translated by Richard Mayne, London: Penguin Press, 1994.

Bronowski, J. and Mazlish, Bruce, *The Western Intellectual Tradition*, New York: Harper and Row Publishers, 1975.

Bullock, Alan, *Hitler and Stalin: Parallel Lives*, London: Fontana Press, 1993.

Burke, Edmund, *Reflections on the Revolution in France*, Oxford: Oxford University Press, 1993.

Chomsky, Noam, *Powers and Prospects*, London: Pluto Press, 1996.

Coates, Austin, *Rizal: Philippines Nationalist and Martyr*, Hong Kong: Oxford University Press, 1988.

*Confucius: The Great Digest, the Unwobbling Pivot, the Analects*, translation and commentary by Ezra Pound, New York: New Directions Books, 1969.

Conrad, Joseph, *Heart of Darkness*, London: Penguin, 1994.

Daniel, Norman, *Islam and the West*, Oxford: Oneworld Publications Ltd, 1993.

Dostoevsky, Fyodor, *Crime and Punishment*, New York: The Modern Library, 1994.

Drucker, Peter, *Post-Capitalist Society*, Oxford: Butterworth-Heinemann Ltd, 1993.

Durant, Will, *The Story of Civilization* , 11 Vols., New York: MJF Books, 1953.

Dutta, Krishna and Robinson, Andrew, *Rabindranath Tagore: The Myriad-Minded Man*, New York: St. Martin's Press, 1995.

Eliot, T.S., *The Complete Poems and Plays (1909–1950)*, Florida: Harcourt Brace and Company, 1980.

Feyerabend, Paul, *Farewell to Reason*, London: Nicholas Brealey Publishing Ltd, 1996.

Friedman, Milton, *Capitalism and Freedom*, Chicago: The University of Chicago Press, 1982.

Friedman, Milton, *Money Mischief Episodes in Monetary History*, New York: Harcourt Brace Jovanovich, 1992.

Friedman, Milton and Rose, *Free to Choose*, San Diego: Harcourt Brace and Company, 1990.

Fromm, Erich, *The Revolution of Hope*, New York: Harper and Row Publishers, 1974.

Galbraith, John Kenneth, *The Culture of Contentment*, London: Sinclair-Stevenson, 1992.

Galbraith, John Kenneth, *A Journey Through Economic Time*, New York: Houghton Mifflin Company, 1994.

Gandhi, Mohandas Karamchand, *The Story of My Experiments with Truth*, London: Cambridge University Press, 1964.

García Márquez, Gabriel, *One Hundred Years of Solitude*, translated by Gregory Rabassa, London: Pan Books Ltd, 1978.

García Márquez, Gabriel, *The General in His Labyrinth*, translated by Edith Grossman, London: Jonathan Cape, 1991.

Gasset, José Ortega y, *The Revolt of the Masses*, Indiana: The University of Notre Dame Press, 1985.

Gellner, Ernest, *Condition of Liberty: Civil Society and Its Rivals*, London: Hamish Hamilton, 1994.

Gilson, Etienne, *Dante and Philosophy*, translated by David Moore, New York: Harper and Row, 1963.

Gordimer, Nadine, *The Lying Days*, London: Penguin Books, 1994.

Hardy, Thomas, *Tess of the D'Urbervilles*, Middlesex: Penguin Books, 1979.

Hayek, F.A., *The Road to Serfdom*, Chicago: University of Chicago Press, 1972.

Heilbroner, Robert, *Twenty-First Century Capitalism*, New York: W.W. Norton and Company, Inc., 1994.

Hemingway, Ernest, *The Essential Hemingway*, Great Britain: Granada Publishing Ltd, 1981.

Herrnstein, Richard J. and Murray, Charles, *The Bell Curve: Intelligence and Class Structure in American Life*, New York: The Free Press, 1994.

Hobsbawm, Eric, *Age of Extremes: The Short 20th Century 1914–1991*, London: Michael Joseph, 1994.

Hodgson, Marshall G.S., *Rethinking World History*, Cambridge: Cambridge University Press, 1993.

Holmes, Oliver Wendell, *The Common Law*, edited by Mark Dewolfe Howe, Boston: Little, Brown and Company, 1963.

Howard, Philip K., *The Death of Common Sense*, New York: Random House, 1994.

Hughes, Robert, *Culture of Complaint*, London: HarperCollins Publishers, 1994.

Ibn Taymiya, Al-Shaykh Al-Imam, *Public Duties in Islam*, translated by Muhtar Holland, Leicester: The Islamic Foundation, 1985.

Iqbal, Muhammad, *The Reconstruction of Religious Thought in Islam*, edited and annotated by Sheikh Muhammad Ashraf, Lahore: Sh. Muhammad Ashraf, 1958.

Iqbal, Muhammad, *The Mysteries of Selflessness*, translated by Arthur J. Arberry, London: John Murray Ltd, 1953.

Iqbal, Muhammad, *The Secrets of the Self*, translation and notes by R.A. Nicholson, Lahore: Sh. Muhammad Ashraf, 1972.

Ishiguro, Kazuo, *The Remains of the Day*, London: Faber and Faber, 1993.

*Islamization of Knowledge*, Virginia: International Institute of Islamic Thought, 1989.

James, Henry, *The Wings of the Dove*, Middlesex: Penguin Books, 1976.

Johnson, Paul, *Modern Times*, London: Phoenix, 1992.

Joyce, James, *Ulysses*, London: Penguin Books, 1992.

Kafka, Franz, *Letters to Friends, Family and Editors*, translated by Richard and Clara Winston, London: John Calder, 1978.

Kafka, Franz, *The Trial*, translated by Willa and Adwin Muir, New York: Schocken Books, 1984.

Kagan, Donald, *On the Origins of War*, New York: Bantam Doubleday Dell Publishing Group, Inc., 1995.

Kamali, Mohamad Hashim, *Principles of Islamic Jurisprudence*, Cambridge: Islamic Texts Society, 1991.

Kawabata, Yasunari, *Snow Country and Thousand Cranes*, translated by Edward G. Seidensticker, London: Penguin Books, 1971.

Khadduri, Majid, *Islamic Jurisprudence: Al Shafi'is Risalah*, Baltimore: Johns Hopkins Press, 1961.

King, Alexander and Schneider, Bertrand, *The First Global Revolution*, London: Simon and Schuster, 1991.

Krugman, Paul R., *Peddling Prosperity*, New York: W.W. Norton and Co., 1994.

Lady Murasaki, *The Tale of Genji*, translated by Arthur Waley, New York: The Modern Library, 1993.

Locke, John, *Two Treatises of Government*, edited by Peter Laslett, New York: Mentor, 1965.

Lu Xun, *Selected Works*, 4 Vols., Beijing: Foreign Languages Press, 1956.

M. Ramlan (trans.), *Babad Tanah Jawa*, Kuala Lumpur: DBP, 1975.

Madison, James, Alexander, Hamilton and John, Jay, *The Federalist Papers*, edited by Clinton Rossiter, New York: New American Library, 1961.

Mahathir bin Mohamad, *The Malay Dilemma*, Singapore: Donald Moore for Asia Pacific Press, 1970.

Majul, Cesar Adib, *Political and Constitutional Ideas of the Philippines Revolution*, Manila: University of the Philippines Press, 1967.

Makdisi, George, *The Rise of Humanism in Classical Islam and the Christian West*, Edinburgh: Edinburgh University Press, 1980.

Mann, Thomas, *Buddenbrooks*, translated from the German by H.T. Lowe-Porter, New York: Afred A. Knopf, 1955.

Mazrui, Ali Al'Amin, *Cultural Forces in World Politics*, London: James Currey, 1990.

Meadows, Donella H., Meadows, Dennis L., Randers, Jorgen, W. Behreeus III, William, *The Limits to Growth, A Report for the Club of Rome's Project on the Predicament of Mankind*, London: Pan Books Ltd, 1972.

*Mencius*, translated by D.C. Lau, London: Penguin Books, 1988.

Mill, John Stuart, *On Liberty*, in *Great Books of the World Vol. 40*, edited by Mortimer J. Adler, Chicago: Encyclopaedia Britannica, Inc., 1991.

Muruyama, Masao, *Studies in the Intellectual History of Tokugawa Japan*, translated by Mikiso Hane, Tokyo: University of Tokyo Press, 1974.

Naqvi, S.N.H., *Ethics and Economics: An Islamic Synthesis*, London: The Islamic Foundation, 1981.

Nasr, Seyyed Hossein, *The Encounter of Man and Nature, The Spiritual Crisis of Modern Man*, London: George Allen and Unwin Ltd, 1968.

Nasr, Seyyed Hossein and Leaman, Oliver, *History of Islamic Philosophy*, 2 Vols., London: Routledge, 1996.

Needham, Joseph, *The Shorter Science and Civilization in China*, 4 Vols., Cambridge: Cambridge University Press, 1978.

Negroponte, Nicholas, *Being Digital*, New York: Alfred A. Knopf, 1995.

Niebuhr, Reinhold, *The Children of Light and the Children of Darkness*, New York: Charles Scribner's Sons, 1960.

Nietzsche, Friedrich, *Beyond Good and Evil*, London: Penguin Books, 1993.

Novak, Michael, *The Spirit of Democratic Capitalism*, New York: Madison Books, 1991.

Paular, Regino P. (ed.), *Rizal as an Internationalist*, Manila: National Historical Institute, 1992.

Popper, Karl Raimund, Sir, *The Open Society and Its Enemies*, Taipei: Rainbow-Bridge Book, 1966.

Popper, Karl Raimund, Sir, *The Logic of Scientific Discovery*, London: Hutchinson, 1977.

Postman, Neil, *Technology*, New York: Random House, Inc., 1993.

Pound, Ezra, *The Cantos*, London: Faber and Faber Ltd, 1990.

Rahman, Fazlur, *Islam and Modernity*, Chicago: The University of Chicago Press, 1982.

Rawls, John, *A Theory of Justice*, Cambridge: Harvard University Press, 1971.

Rizal, José, *Noli Me Tangere*, translated by M.A. Soledad Lacson-Locsin, edited by Paul L. Locsin, Makati City: Bookmark, 1996.

Rosenthal, Franz, *Knowledge Triumphant*, Leiden: E.J. Brill, 1970.

Said, Edward W., *Orientalism*, London: Routledge and Kegan Paul, 1978.

Said, Edward W., *Culture and Imperialism*, New York: Vintage, 1994.

Schumacher, E.R., *A Guide for the Perplexed*, Middlesex: Penguin Books Ltd, 1989.

Shakespeare, *The Globe Illustrated Shakespeare*, New Jersey: Gramercy Books, 1993.

Shellabear, W.G. (ed.), *Sejarah Melayu*, Kuala Lumpur: Oxford University Press, 1967.

Skidelsky, Robert, *John Maynard Keynes: The Economist As Saviour 1920–1937*, London: Penguin Press, 1994.

Skidelsky, Robert, *The World After Communism*, London: Macmillan, 1995.

Smith, Adam, *The Theory of Moral Sentiments*, edited by D.D. Raphael and A.L. Macfie, Oxford: Clarendon Press, 1976.

Smith, Huston, *The Religions of Man*, New York: Harper and Row, 1986.

Snow, C.P., *Corridors of Power*, New York: Charles Scribner's Sons, 1964.

Spengler, Oswald, *The Decline of the West*, London: George Allen and Unwin, 1980.

Tagore, Rabindranath, *Collected Poems and Plays*, London: Macmillan London Ltd, 1988.

Tapscott, Don, *The Digital Economy*, New York: McGraw-Hill, 1996.

*The Holy Quran*, text, translation and commentary by Abdullah Yusuf Ali, Maryland: Amana Corporation, 1989.

Thurow, Lester, *The Future of Capitalism*, London: Nicholas Brealey Publishing Ltd, 1996.

Tocqueville, Alexis de, *Democracy in America*, 2 Vols., New York: Alfred A. Knopf, 1963.

Tolstoy, Leo, *Great Short Works of Leo Tolstoy*, New York: Perennial Library, 1967.

Toynbee, Arnold J., *The Word and the West*, London: Oxford University Press, 1953.

Tsunoda, R. Yusaku, de Bary, Wm Theodore and Keene, Donald, *Sources of Japanese Tradition*, 2 Vols., New York: Columbia University Press, 1964.

Wiesl, Elie, *Night, Dawn, The Accident Three Tales*, London: Robson Books Ltd, 1987.

Wilson, James Q., *The Moral Sense*, New York: The Free Press, 1993.

# Index

# About the Author

Anwar Ibrahim is Deputy Prime Minister and Finance Minister of Malaysia. He is also president of the International Islamic University, Malaysia, and has served as president of the General Assembly of UNESCO. Since 1982, he has held several Cabinet portfolios, including that of Culture, Youth and Sports, Agriculture and Education.

He is deputy president of UMNO (the United Malays National Organization), the dominant party in the ruling Barisan Nasional coalition.

He was born in Penang in 1947. He is married to Dr Wan Azizah Wan Ismail. They have six children.